alg

Compact Guide: Algarve tells you all you need to know about Portugal's southern coastline, from wild and windy Sagres in the west to the calm lagoons of Tavira in the east, from quiet fishing villages to showcase resorts, and from Moorish castles to baroque churches filled with gilt carvings and dazzling *azulejos*.

This is one of more than 80 titles in *Apa Publications'* new series of pocket-sized, easy-to-use guidebooks intended for the independent-minded traveller. *Compact Guides* are in essence travel encyclopedias in miniature, designed to be comprehensive yet portable, as well as up-to-date and authoritative.

D'AFONSO III
1210-1279

Star Attractions

An instant reference to some of the Algarve's most popular tourist attractions to help you on your way.

Faro Old Town p19

Lagos fort p26

Museu Municipal de José Formosinho p27

Igreja de Santo Antonio p27

Sagres' Villa do Infante p 29

Cabo de São Vicente p30

Praia da Rocha p36

Loulé market p43

Vila Romana de Milréu p50

Tavira p51

Temple of Diana p57

algarve

Al-Gharb – The Land in the West

Al-Gharb was the Arab name for the southernmost province of Portugal when it was part of the Moorish kingdom. The Arabs left, but the name remained – indeed, Moorish influence is still everywhere in evidence. The almond, fig and carob trees which the Arabs introduced are integral features of the landscape. Around two-thirds of the place names in Algarve have the Arab prefix *al*. The cube-like architecture characteristic of places such as Olhão are extremely reminiscent of a North African casbah. Even the wind from the Sahara caresses the south Portuguese coast.

A fine perch

'Algarve isn't Portugal', goes a saying. For the Portuguese, the extreme end of their country was always considered a strange land. Even King Alphonse III styled himself *Rei de Portugal e do Algarve* after his victory over the Moors in 1249. The place has always been very different from the rest of Portugal – in the past because it was ruled by the Moors for so long, and today because tourism has changed it so much.

Tourism is still bringing changes to the region. New construction extends into the very smallest bay, and along the western part of the coast in particular every fishing village has been transformed into a tourist resort. The brightly coloured fishing boats on the beaches are almost the only reminder of the villages' former quiet charms, and even these are left there to appeal to the tourists. To see the real Algarve, with its whitewashed houses contrasting attractively with the terracotta-coloured earth, you need to travel inland. That's also the only place to find the farmers' two-wheeled donkey carts (*carrinhas*). Inland you will find no trace of the prosperity that tourism has brought to the coast.

When the donkey work is over

Position and size

Portugal is the westernmost country in Europe and also one of the smallest, with a total surface area of just 92,389sq km (35,670sq miles). The Algarve accounts for 5.6 percent of Portugal, covering 4,960sq km (1,900sq miles). Its beautiful and varied south coast is more than 150km (93 miles) long and comprises bays, sandy beaches, lagoons, marshes and sand dunes. The steep cliffs along the west coast extend 40km (24 miles), and are broken only by the odd stretch of sandy beach. The whole of the Algarve coastline is washed by the Atlantic Ocean – the Mediterranean lies beyond the Straits of Gibraltar.

Geographically, the Algarve and North Africa are next-door neighbours. It's just a stone's throw

Serra de Alcaria do Cume

from the south coast of Portugal to Morocco. In the east the Rio Guadiana forms the border with Spain, and in the north the province of Alentejolies lies beyond a mountain range. The tallest peaks are Foía (902m/2,959ft) in the Serra de Monchique, the Miradouro do Caldeirão (545m/1,788ft) in the Serra do Caldeirão, and the Serra de Alcaria do Cume (525m/1,722ft) in the mountain range of the same name. Geologically, the Algarve has two separate sections: the mountains to the north and the narrow coastal strips, composed mainly of limestone sediment, to the south. On the map, the EN125 – the Algarve's main traffic artery – seems to separate these two very different landscapes. The Portuguese divide the province into three regions: *serra* (mountains), *barrocal* (hill country) and *costa* (coast). The region is irrigated by just a few small streams, which are often nothing more than dried-up wadis. The larger among them include the Rio Arade, which reaches the sea near Portimão, and the Rio Guadiana which separates Portugal from Spain.

Praia da Rocha

Coasts and beaches

Europe's southernmost point is the Cabo de São Vicente. Mariners used to refer to it as *o Fim do Mundo* (the World's End), and no-one ever dared lose sight of it on the horizon until Henry the Navigator arrived on the scene and put an end to this idea. The south coast of the Algarve is made up of two completely different terrains. The Barlovento, situated between Sagres and Quarteira, has bizarre-looking rock formations and attractive bays with sandy beaches. The cliffs extend like tentacles into the greenish-blue waters of the Atlantic. Wind and water have cut impressive pillars, arches and other shapes out of the calcareous sandstone – creating strange forms reminiscent of fairytale creatures.

The stretch of coast known as the Sotavento extends from Quarteira as far as the Guadiana. It's an absolutely flat region with dunes, lagoons and sandbanks. The sandy beaches here extend as far as the eye can see.

Leaving footprints in the sand

When to go

The Algarve has a pleasant, Mediterranean climate influenced by Africa. In July and August the daily temperatures often exceed 35°C (95°F), and in winter they fluctuate between 15°C (59°F) and 22°C (71°F) with an occasional spell of heavy rain. Along the western coastline there's almost always a fresh cool wind blowing, known as the *nortadas*, and the evenings there can get quite cold. From time to time a heavy fog descends on the west coast – but it disappears almost as soon as it arrives.

The Algarve is sunny in winter, so the coast can be visited all year round. For beach holidays, the best time to go is between May and October. June is a particularly beautiful month: many plants are in bloom, and oranges hang from the trees. The famous almond blossom appears in February. Take along summer clothing, but also pack a warm jacket to protect against cool winds and to wear inside when the air conditioning is set over high.

Nature and the environment

The Algarve is also known as the Garden of Portugal. An incredible variety of fruit grows here: oranges, lemons, figs, melons, peaches, plums, carobs (*alfarroba*), delicious small yellow fruits known as medlars (*nêsperas*), quinces and pomegranates. The mild climate and the fertile soil have created a fascinating natural landscape containing several different zones of vegetation. Along the coast, the red earth and the cacti, agaves and rock roses are all reminiscent of a desert landscape; only the white and pink oleander bushes provide welcome splashes of colour. The *barrocal* is an important agricultural area. Wheat, beans, tomatoes and vines are all grown in abundance here. Olive groves (*oliveiras*), pine (*piheiros*), fir (*piheiros bravos*), eucalyptus, cork (*sobreiros*) and chestnut oak (*azinheiros*) all grow along the slopes higher up.

Flowers and fruit thrive

Around 200 species of fish swim off the coast of southern Portugal, and although their numbers are dwindling, the most common is still the sardine. In former days the sardine fishermen were assisted in their work by the *cáo d'agua* (*see pages 9 and 49*). This Portuguese breed of dog is black, furry and not unlike a poodle in appearance – except that it has 'webbed paws', which permit it to swim exceptionally well.

Another Portuguese breed of dog is the *perdigáo*, which may be distantly related to the shorthair terrier. There are also two Portuguese horse breeds: *Lusitano* and *Alter Real*. Their courage and manoeuvrability makes them ideal for use in bullfighting. Donkeys and mules are still a common sight in the more rural areas. Wild animals abound in the Algarve, and you may even be lucky enough to spot a chameleon. Storks are also common. Their nests on the top of high buildings are very much a part of the local scenery. The Algarve is also a popular stopover for birds flying to and from Africa.

At home in the Algarve

The Algarve contains several nature reserves, including the Parque Natural da Ria Formosa (a land and seascape dotted with islands between Faro and Tavira), the Reserva Natural de Castro Marim on the Spanish border and the Reserva Natural da Costa Vicentina, which takes up practically the entire west coast from Cabo de São Vicente as far as the Alentejo. No construction activity is permitted in any of these areas. Although ecologists and environmental activists are still considered weak and

7

On the green

Bridge to Spain

Fresh water, a scarce resource

ineffectual idealists by many Portuguese, they have succeeded in getting their own way in the Algarve. Nevertheless, progressively dry weather conditions are gradually creating crisis conditions in southern Portugal. Public and private wells are having to be drilled deeper and deeper. The groundwater level has sunk so deep in some places that salty seawater is penetrating the rock strata several kilometres inland.

Most of the water that is available is piped to hotels and golf courses to keep the tourists happy. Hotels that want to keep up with the competition are obliged to provide freshwater swimming pools for their guests. Every tourist – and there are about a million each year – consumes an average of 200 litres of water per day. That is four times as much water as the locals use. However, there are more causes of the depletion in water supply than simple over-consumption by tourists, including climatic changes and antiquated irrigation methods. This region has a long history of water shortages. It was only the construction of reservoirs that led to the belief that water was available in unlimited quantities.

An international squabble has started over who owns the rivers. Neighbouring Spain has even worse water problems than Portugal. New reservoirs along the border are supposed to be helping, but Madrid knows that Portugal gets two-thirds of its water from the rivers. Portugal's problem is that the three main rivers – the Douro, the Tejo and the Guadiana – all have their sources in Spain. Consequently the government in Lisbon has been protesting vehemently about Spain's plans for more reservoirs. But Spain is in a more powerful position. Attempts to resolve the dispute have been going on since 1993. Portugal's Alqueva dam on the Guadiana is the largest hydroelectric project on the Iberian Peninsula – the reservoir is half

as big as Lake Geneva. Spain has decided not to allow the Portuguese the amount of water they need, so the project is already a massive flop. With 3,000 hours of sunshine a year, Portugal would be the ideal place for solar energy – but the technology has to be financed. In the industrial centres, the EU limitations on emissions are regularly exceeded, and agriculture isn't as ecologically sound as it could be. Although it is well-known that eucalyptus drains soil and destroys it, large plantations are appearing, subsidised by the EU. 'Eucalyptus instead of cork and olives' is the new slogan. And as in all poorer countries, what little money there is gets invested in industry rather than ecological projects.

Eucalyptus

Portugal's famous shaggy dog

The *cáo d'agua* is a furry poodle-like dog with webbed paws. The webbed parts have receded somewhat these days, however, since the animal is no longer used for fishing. The *cáo d'agua* is one of the oldest breeds of dog in the world, and it is valued for its intelligence, loyalty and obedience.

9

When most of Portugal's population earned a living fishing, the *cáo d'agua* was a regular sight along the coast. It was the fishermen's constant companion. The dog dived as deep as 4m (13ft) below the surface of the sea, drove the fish into the net and then carried them back to its owner just like a hunting dog – the difference of course being that the whole procedure took place underwater. A membrane inside the dog's mouth prevented it from swallowing too much water.

This seaworthy animal probably took part in several of the great discovery voyages – and may even have saved the odd mariner from drowning. Unfortunately, modern fishing methods and the use of machinery put the animal out of a job. In 1930 Vasco Bensaúde, a ship-owner from the Algarve, began looking after the few remaining Portuguese water poodles to save them from extinction. In the Ria Formosa National Park near Olhão there is a breeding station for the dogs (*see page 49*). Around 1,000 fishing dogs still live in Portugal.

The people

The demographics in the Algarve have seen major changes recently. In 1970, the population was 268,000; by 1991 this figure had risen to 340,000 – 3.4 percent of Portugal's population. However, the rise was localised. In the same period the population density on the Algarve coast rose from 54 to 67 people per sq km, but in the *barrocal* the population fell from 24 percent of the Algarve total to 21 percent. The mountain regions are also emptying at an astonishing rate. In 1960, 70,000 people lived in the

Young Algarvios

Moorish–looking songstress

mountains. Today, there are only around 40,000 people remaining here.

The *Algarvios* are an ethnic mix of Celtic Lusitanians, Romans, Moors and other Africans. The connection with North Africa is evident in their dark skin, almond-shaped eyes and Moorish lifestyle. The Algarve was long considered to be a land of *mais ou menos* – wait and be patient, but this characteristic seems to have been largely dispelled by tourism. Sometimes the *Algarvios* seem very quiet and almost absent-minded, but in conversation they quickly loosen up and are invariably very hospitable, inviting guests to join them for a coffee or a *medronho* – a spirit distilled from the fruit of the strawberry tree.

School's out

Education

Portugal has a long tradition of education – one of the first universities in Europe was founded in Coimbra in the year 1288. Today, however, it has the worst illiteracy rate (15 percent) of any European country. It was only from 1974 that the constitution guaranteed education for all and knowledge ceased to be a luxury. A minimum of nine years at school became compulsory in the early 1990s. Children in rural areas are still at a disadvantage, however: a lack of teachers, closure of the smaller schools and poor transport are all hampering efforts to provide good education nationwide.

Language

Worldwide, 180 million people speak Portuguese – and most of them are Brazilian. The vocabulary and the grammar are based mainly on Latin, but the Arab past has also left traces. The Portuguese word for an olive tree is the Latin-based *oliveira*, but its fruit is the Arab-based *azeitona*, and olive oil is known as *azeite*. Standard Portuguese is based on the dialect of Lisbon, and the dialect spoken in the Algarve is very similar. The language is often mutually intelligible with Spanish despite differences in phonology, grammar and vocabulary. The main differences are the nasal twang of the language, and the small wavy line (~) over some letters.

Church-going is still important

Religion

Portugal is nine-tenths Roman Catholic. There are also 38,000 Protestants, 15,000 Muslims and 2,000 Jews. In the south of the country, Christianity has traditionally been less influential because the area was ruled by the Moors for such a long time. In recent years, religious belief has also been eroded by the influence of tourism and the media. Nevertheless the *santos populares*, Portugal's folk saints, still play an important role in helping and protecting the sick. Even in the main tourist areas of the Algarve almost every family has a patron saint who is treated like one of the family. If these saints fulfil their protective duties they gets praised; if they fail their statues are immersed in water briefly as a punishment, or broken outright, in which case they have to prove themselves again.

The Algarve abounds in saints and spirits of all kinds. With their fates tied so closely to supernatural phenomena, the villagers shouldn't really get out of bed in the mornings at all. For instance, many houses have a blue stripe around them to ward off evil spirits. During pregnancy, women are not allowed to hold a needle and thread for fear of giving birth to a malformed baby. Cat hair is considered powerful magic, and fear of the 'evil eye' is very widespread: it makes people sick and can even lead to death. Anyone who suffers from the *mau olhado* can only be saved by mysterious herbal mixtures.

Someone to watch over you

Economy

Tourism is the biggest hope for Portugal's weak economy. It was the only reason the country's GDP registered an increase after the recession that hit the country at the beginning of the 1990s. Tourism in Portugal centres on the coast of the Algarve, and this tiny region brings in 40 percent of the nation's revenue. At the moment there are 81,000 hotel rooms in the Algarve, compared with second-place Lisbon's 38,000.

The first big crisis in Portugal's booming tourist industry came in 1993 and was caused by the combination of economic recession and a drop in visitor figures. Many hotels, restaurants and bars had to close down, and unemployment in the region rose to 12 percent. All that is past history now, however: some 1.5 million visitors from all over the world land at Faro Airport each year. A good half of them come from Great Britain, and another 20 percent from Germany. The largest group of Algarve short-stay holidaymakers are the Spanish: around 6.5 million of Portugal's (unloved) Spanish neighbours cross the border each year.

11

Great escapes

Traditionally, the Algarve is an agricultural region, and the Arabs contributed much to this by introducing almonds, figs and carobs (*alfarobeirra*). They also introduced various methods of irrigation, and watermills can still be seen here and there, together with wheels powered by mules that also raise water.

Today, agriculture in the Algarve is even more dependent on artificial irrigation because large plantations have been created to grow kiwi fruit, strawberries and asparagus, all of which are harvested year round. Since the early 1990s, over a million orange trees have been planted, covering over 3,000 hectares (7,400 acres) – each of these trees uses 100 litres of water a day. Almond and carob trees

would be far more suitable for the climate. The climate and soil are perfect for intensive agriculture, but the possibilities are not being exploited because the Algarve has placed tourism at the top of its list of priorities.

Traditional agriculture is on the wane, for several reasons. Formerly the children used to help their parents in the fields; today many leave for the towns and tourist centres as soon as they can to earn more and work less. The old-style agriculture is no longer competitive. The many deserted farms inland from the coast are a clear indication of this. The farmers' biggest problem, however, is the EU. They cannot understand why their delicious oranges are not accepted by the international market. Brussels approved oranges have to be round and look attractive – how they taste is of secondary importance to their appearance. The European Union is not too popular in Portugal at present.

A fisherman inspects his nets

The fishing industry is also having problems. Portuguese waters have been overfished, and the tuna have long since disappeared. Now the fishermen concentrate mainly on sardines, whose numbers are also dwindling. The main problem, however, is that no-one is buying sardines any more. Of the 60 or so fish-canning factories in the Algarve, only seven remain. What's more, Spain's fishing fleets are better equipped and more modern, though by 1999 Portugal will have received £210 million worth of subsidies to modernise its fishing industry.

Politics and administration

Electioneering

Two events changed the face of Portugal decisively during recent years: the 'Carnation Revolution' of 1974 brought democracy, and the country's entry into the EU in 1986 brought economic prosperity. Although it was President Mario Soares (Partido Socialista, PS) who signed the contract to join the EU, most of the glory was garnered by former prime minister Anibal Cavaco Silva (Social Democrats, PSD). Cavaco's main achievement was the introduction of political stability. In office from 1985 to 1995, he was the longest-serving head of state in the history of the Portuguese Republic. His policies became increasingly authoritarian, however, and in October 1995 the Socialists won a clear majority. The new head of government is presently 46-year-old Antonio Guterres. Silva has also been succeeded as head of the Social Democratic opposition by Fernando Nogueira, a pragmatist without much charisma.

The *Algarvios* suffer from Portugal's political centralism. The regions subordinate to Lisbon always have to refer to ministries in the capital. Politically, the south of the country is traditionally 'red': 10 of the 16 mayors in the Algarve are members of the PS. Nevertheless, in its role as the country's major tourist centre it is essential to the national economy, so the Algarve enjoys special status in several respects.

Cork

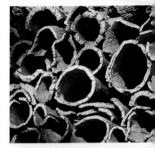

Cork, an economic staple

Cork is a staple of the Portuguese economy – one-third of the world's cork oaks (*sobreiros*) grow here. Attempts to cultivate the trees in California or the Ukraine have so far proved fruitless. This leaves Portugal as the world's largest cork exporter. Business is getting harder these days, however, because synthetic products are increasingly replacing the genuine article. Bottles with plastic or screw tops are growing more common even in Portugal, the centre of the industry.

Cork production is a complex business. The bark of the cork trees is partially pared off at regular intervals timed to give the tree time to regenerate. The bare trunk is then daubed with a dark-brown solution to protect it. The bark is then washed and boiled to rid it of vermin and mineral salts. The lightweight cork has to be kept underwater throughout this process. The high temperature makes the cells in the bark expand, giving the cork its elasticity. The great advantage of cork is that it is light, waterproof and almost completely airtight.

A harvested tree

13

Henry the Navigator

Henrique (Henry), the third son of King João I and Philippa (daughter of John of Gaunt), was born in 1394, just as Portugal had finished an exhausting war against Spain. Intimidated by the enemy on its doorstep, and almost bankrupt because of the cost of the war, Portugal was forced to turn its attention to the sea and seafaring as a way of keeping its out-of-work soldiers occupied.

With no hope of gaining the crown and sceptre, the Infante Dom Henrique decided to steer Portugal out of its economic crisis instead. His ambition was to find a sea route to India in order to gain a large proportion of the trade in spices, silks and luxury goods from the Far East. Until then, this trade had been under the almost exclusive dominion of Arabs and Venetians. Here the Prince clearly demonstrated his pioneering spirit.

Statue of Henry the Navigator

Henry's nickname 'The Navigator' should not be taken too literally. In 1415, having only just come of age, he went on his first and probably only sea voyage, joining the fleet of warships with red crosses on their sails that captured Ceuta in Morocco. The collapse of Ceuta marked the end of the North African trading monopoly, and the foundation-stone for European expansion was laid. Portugal prepared to take its place among the world powers.

The enterprise was organised and financed by the Order of Christ, of which Henry was made grand master in

1420. At the age of 25 he was already governor of the Algarve and supreme commander of most of the Portuguese fleet. In 1433 he secured a monopoly on soap and tuna fish, and in 1443 he gained control of all sea traffic and trade with newly-discovered countries beyond the Cabo Bojador. These lands fell to the Crown, but Henry received one-fifth (*quinto*) of all the proceeds from trade in gold, spices and slaves. He promptly reinvested the money in his maritime undertakings.

While Henry's seamen were gradually penetrating further south along the West African coast, the shipbuilders in Lagos were manufacturing an entirely new vessel: the Portuguese caravel, the first ship that could sail against the wind. This masterly technical achievement made possible the voyages of discovery, and caravels were used almost exclusively after Gil Eanes successfully passed the Cabo Bojador in 1434.

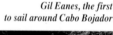

Gil Eanes, the first to sail around Cabo Bojador

Henry carefully gathered together all the available knowledge about seafaring, sea routes, etc and created a kind of nautical research centre. This contained a further development of the Arab astrolabe, an important instrument for determining latitude from the position of the stars. The armillary sphere, which depicted the most important sections of the heavens, also developed from this, and it came to symbolise Portuguese seafaring and discovery from the 15th century onwards.

Henry was very careful to guard his hard-won navigating knowledge. The penalty for illegally disseminating nautical know-how at that time was death. Maritime maps were particularly closely guarded. Henry died in 1460, and his fame rests primarily on his patronage of navigators. For this he is justly regarded as the initiator of the great Age of Discovery, which set the Europeans on the road to world domination.

The former slave market, Lagos

Historical Highlights

From 1000BC Celts and Carthaginians settle the Iberian Peninsula.

From 218BC Roman troops expel the Carthaginians. In 133BC Lusitania becomes a province of the Roman Empire.

AD711 Islamic armies from Africa invade the Iberian Peninsula and conquer it almost immediately. Xelb (Silves) becomes the capital of the Moorish kingdom.

725 The *Reconquista* by the Christians begins.

1095 Count Henry of Burgundy is granted the county of Portucale.

1139 Henry's son Afonso Henriques defeats the Moors near Ourique (Beja) and styles himself King of Portugal. In 1179 Pope Alexander III recognises Portugal's independence in return for a yearly tribute.

1189 King Sancho I captures Silves and destroys the Moors' former capital. The Moors win it back after another two years of fighting.

1249 The Moors are finally driven from Algarve by Afonso III. The *Reconquista* is over.

1383 Fernando I dies, bringing to an end the male line of the House of Burgundy. Fernando's son-in-law, Juan I of Castile, lays claim to the throne of Portugal. The population rebels and declares João from the House of Avis as their king.

1415 Henry the Navigator sets sail from Lagos to conquer Ceuta, a major trading centre in Morocco. Lagos becomes the starting point for the great voyages of discovery.

1494 In the Treaty of Tordesillas, Pope Alexander VI divides the world into spheres of Portuguese and Spanish interest.

1498 Vasco da Gama discovers the sea route to India. Two years later, Pedro Alvares Cabral reaches Brazil.

1519–22 The first circumnavigation of the globe is completed by Fernáo de Magalháes.

1578 King Sebastião sets sail from Lagos with over 800 caravels to capture Morocco. He suffers a disastrous defeat and Portugal's resources are drained to pay ransoms.

1580 Philip II of Spain becomes Philip I of Portugal, promising to maintain Portugal's autonomy within the new union.

1640 The Duke of Bragança defeats the Spanish and is crowned King João IV.

1755 The whole of Portugal is shaken by a severe earthquake on All Saints' Day.

1807–14 Napoleon occupies Portugal three times. The Portuguese court escapes to Brazil.

1814–20 A British army liberates Portugal. Lord Beresford declares Portugal a protectorate.

1822 The Liberal Revolution replaces the English with King João VI, who is forced to accept a constitution.

1910 The Republic is proclaimed.

1928 Antonio de Salazar becomes minister of finance; four years later he becomes president; in 1933 he sets up his Estado Novo dictatorship.

1961 Wars of independence begin in Portugal's African colonies.

1974 The left-wing Carnation Revolution ends the dictatorship without bloodshed.

1975 Portugal's former African colonies gain their independence.

1976 The Partido Socialista (PS) becomes the most powerful party in Portugal.

1986 Portugal joins the EC.

1989 The classless society clause is removed from the constitution as a national aim, thus paving the way for privatisation.

1995 The Socialists win the elections. Antonio Guterres becomes president of Portugal.

Arxco de Repouso
Preceding pages: view of Albufeira

A quiet corner and a bustling café

Route 1

Faro

Capital of the Algarve

Those arriving at ★ Faro by plane often admire the beautiful little islands and beaches along the Ria Formosa, but once they've moved on to their holiday resort, they very rarely budge. That is Faro's problem: tourists usually pass through its airport – opened in 1965 – on their way to Albufeira, Armaçáo de Pêra or Praia da Rocha – and never come back to explore.

In a way it's fortunate that the capital of the Algarve is passed over so often, because it has thus managed to retain its own special, very Portuguese charm. Its beaches are another matter, however. The local beach, Praia de Faro, is right next to the airport and has no appeal whatsoever, though there are beautiful sandy beaches further eastwards. Faro lies at the junction of two very different types of coastline: the Barlovento in the west, with its bays and small beaches, and the Sotavento to the east, where long sandy beaches extend to the Spanish border.

If you can bear to leave the beach for a day without sunbathing, maybe to go shopping or to see a few sights, Faro is definitely the place to go. The town's central pedestrian precinct with its elegant shops and friendly cafés is very lively and busy, but most of Faro's charm comes from its generously laid out parks down by the harbour, with their palm trees and lawns. It's advisable to set off in the early morning for any visit here, because parking space tends to be very limited any time after 9am. In addition, the priest locks the cathedral at noon, so afternoon visitors will be disappointed.

Today, the capital of the Algarve has a population of 30,000 and is the political, industrial and intellectual centre of the region. The university has more than 6,000 students, who give the town a lively, modern flair that is especially noticeable after sunset.

History

Faro became a metropolis relatively late. When the Romans were here it was known as Ossonoba, and they turned it into an important trading centre. The most important remains dating from that time are the Roman ruins of Milréu (*see page 50*), a few miles outside Faro.

When the town was captured by the Moors in a very fierce war in 714, it was renamed Haro after the victorious Arab tribe of Beni Harun. Over the centuries the name gradually changed to Faro. Under the Moorish prince Ben Said, Faro flourished briefly as a capital city, but after its recapture in 1249 by King Alfonso III it became a sleepy provincial town once more. The Portuguese king, who from then on styled himself 'King of Portugal and Algarve', chose Lagos as his residence instead. Lagos remained the capital until it was completely destroyed in the earthquake of 1755. Faro became the capital again just one year later.

Alfonso III

Faro received its municipal charter as early as 1540, however, and in 1580 the bishop of Silves shifted his episcopal seat to Faro. This was another milestone in the town's growing importance. A few years later, in 1596, Faro experienced large-scale destruction for the first time: at the behest of Queen Elizabeth I it was burned to the ground by the Earl of Essex, despite the fact that England and Portugal had signed a friendship treaty. Two serious earthquakes followed soon afterwards: the first hit Faro in 1722 and devastated half the town, and the population were still clearing up the damage when in 1755 a second quake destroyed not only Faro but every community along the coast as well. That is why most of the town's buildings date from after 1755.

Rambling over the Old City **19**

Arco da Vila

City Tour

Despite the earthquakes some historic buildings still stand, and they give the ★★ **Cidade Velha** ❶ (Old Town) much of its charm. The most attractive and impressive place to start any tour of the town is the ★ **Arco da Vila** ❷ (Town Gate), which leads into the oldest part. This *Vila-a-Dentro* (town within a town) is still surrounded by what is left of the medieval wall. Francisco Gomez de Avelar, bishop and also regent of the province, commissioned the Italian architect Francisco Xavier Fabri to build this very impressive Renaissance gate. In 1812 the structure

To Largo da Sé

was ready, complete with its two Ionic columns. A statue of the town's patron saint, Thomas Aquinas, stands in a niche above the main arch, giving its blessing to all who pass through. The people of Faro paid for the statue as a mark of gratitude for being spared the worst excesses of war, death and the plague, which ravaged the rest of Portugal during the 17th century. A few years ago two storks built their nest above the bell tower on the very top of the gate, and many *Farenses* believe that the town will prosper as long as the birds remain there.

Passing through the Arco da Vila is like entering an entirely different world. Suddenly the bustle of the town ceases, and donkeys and mules are the only traffic in the streets, which are far too narrow for cars. The cobbled road leads to the ★ **Largo da Sé** ❸, a large square laid out after the great earthquake. Indeed, all the houses here were

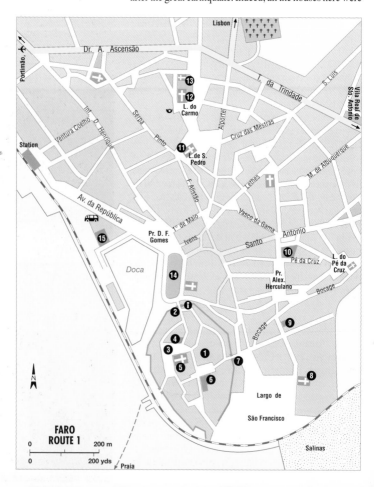

FARO
ROUTE 1

0 —— 200 m
0 —— 200 yds / Praia

built after 1755, and the red-tiled roofs, tall windows and wrought-iron balconies (*verandas de ferro forjado*) give the whole place an attractive harmony and simplicity.

The first building on the right is the Câmara Municipal, or Town Hall. Next door to it is the **Paço Episcopal ④** (Episcopal Palace), a majestic 18th-century building. The walls of the inner courtyard, the magnificent staircase and the three halls inside are all decorated with what are considered the finest ★ *azulejo* tiles in the Algarve. They came from the Fabrica do Rato in Lisbon. Visitor access to the palace is limited, unfortunately, as the bishops are still in residence.

When Faro was made a bishopric by Afonso de Castelo Branco in 1580, the entire clergy moved to Faro and with it came the Seminario Episcopal, or priest's seminary. This structure was also designed by the architect Fabri and commissioned by Bishop Dom Francisco Gomes. The first phase of construction was completed in 1789. The rooftop towers that resemble lighthouses are still used as watchtowers by the *padres* to ensure that the *seminaristas* are behaving themselves.

Cathedral exterior

The main building in the square is the **Sé ⑤** (Cathedral) – *sé* being the abbreviation for the Latin term *sedes episcopalis* (bishop's seat). It probably sits on the ruins of a 13th-century mosque. It has an incredible mixture of styles – Gothic, Renaissance and baroque – which, combined with its lack of any kind of proportion, make it quite fascinating. Nothing fits; there's no trace of architectural unity whatsoever. The mighty bell tower survives from the former Gothic cathedral, and the cathedral's three-aisled interior is entered through one of the three Gothic portals. Renaissance elements here include the Doric columns supporting the barrel vault, the beautiful gold-painted wooden ceiling and the high altar with its *talha* (gilt wood carving; *see page 59*). The **Capela de Nossa Senhora do Rosario** is one of the finest chapels, with plenty of gold decoration and wonderful *azulejos* tiles in the Dutch style depicting the *Flight from Egypt*. Finally, the magnificent and recently restored baroque **organ** is considered to be one of the finest in Portugal.

Decorative detail

Flight from Egypt azulejos

Turn left as you leave the cathedral to reach the Praça Afonso III, named after the king who finally integrated Algarve into Portugal. The ★ **Convento das Clarissas de Nossa Senhora da Assunção ⑥** is praiseworthy for two reasons: firstly because of its architecture and secondly because of its museum. The convent was built in 1543 – the Moorish and baroque appearance of the tower is misleading. Although the building is one of the few in Faro to have survived the English ransacking and the two earthquakes, it failed to withstand the anticlericalism of the Republicans. The nuns were forced to abandon the convent, and it was turned into a cork factory. Restoration work took place only recently, and today it houses both the municipal library and the ★ **Museu Arqueologico e Lapidar Infante Dom Henrique** (Tuesday to Friday 9am–noon and 2–7pm). In the upper cloister, which is one of the finest Renaissance works in all Algarve, there is a row of stone *escudos* (coats of arms) of great interest. Archaeological finds from the Roman ruins of Milréu (*see page 50*) can also be admired, including busts of the empress Agrippina and the emperor Hadrian, and also a very recently discovered 4-m (13-ft) by 11-m (35-ft) floor mosaic. The art collection includes works by Rembrandt and Gauguin and several works by the famous Portuguese portrait painters Antonio de Sequeira (1768–1837) and Columbano Bordalo Pinheiro (1857–1929).

Legend has it that King Afonso III rode with his troops through the **Arco do Repouso ❼** in 1249 to recapture Faro from the Moors. It is called *repouso* (repose) because the king is supposed to have taken a break here from the strains of his victorious campaign before calmly accepting the keys of the city. A modern tile-picture beside the arch depicts a scene from the conquest.

An aptly named thoroughfare

Tile picture of the conquest

The ★ **Igreja de São Francisco ❽** lies on the dusty square of the same name, disfigured by around 1,000 motor vehicles a day. It's worth crossing the square, however, because the church interior is particularly magnificent. Founded by the Franciscan Order at the end of the 17th century, the church lies beside the former monastery (now a barracks) and is famed for its *talha dourada* (*see page 59*) as well as its masterly *azulejo* panels. The tiles show scenes from the life of St Francis. The walls and the dome are faced with valuable gilt carvings, making one wonder how the craftsmen ever managed to get their work up there. In the former monastery garden there's another surprise: a hexagonal granary (*celeiro*) of a kind only ever seen in Northern Portugal. Its walls are covered with basreliefs depicting mythological figures.

Continue northwards as far as the **Palacio Belmarço ❾**, which was built by the architect Norte Junior in 1917. It must have been quite a fairytale palace when first built, but today its former splendour can only be guessed at. Unfortunately the whole place is gradually falling apart because no money is available to save it.

A rewarding detour can be made from here to the ★★ **Museu Etnografico Regional ❿** (Monday to Friday 9.30am–12.30pm and 2–5.30pm) inside the regional administration building known as the Assembleia Distrital. The exhibits centre around the traditional everyday life of farmers, fishermen and craftsmen. The Faro artist Carlos Porfirio, a friend of Picasso, assembled the numerous examples of local craftsmanship on display, including

Igreja do Carmo

basketwork, embroidery, cork products and carpets. There is also a fascinating exhibition on the architecture of the typical farmhouse of the Algarve, the *casa algarvia*, including a convincing replica.

If you carry straight on, rather than turning into the Rua de Santo Antonio, you'll end up in the busy centre of Faro with all its cafés, restaurants and pedestrian precincts. Don't forget to look up occasionally: now and then you'll see a very fine facade with the *janelas de guilhotina* (guillotine windows) and *verandas de ferro forjado* (wrought-iron balconies) that are so typical of this part of Portugal.

Skip the shopping for the time being: two churches further north are worth a visit. The first is the **Igreja de São Pedro ⑪**, which dates from the 16th century and was originally a small fishermen's chapel. Those pressed for time can just admire its superb Renaissance portal without going inside. Those who enter will find several artistic highlights in the three-aisled interior: some fine *talha dourada*, an *azulejo* panel in the right transept, a bas-relief of *The Last Supper* dating from the 18th century, and a portrait of St Anna attributed to the baroque artist Machado de Castro, famed in Portugal for his crib scenes.

The detour to the next church takes about 15 minutes, but is worthwhile, especially for fans of gilt baroque ornamentation. The Carmelites came to Faro early in the 18th century, and in 1713 they built the massive ★★ **Igreja do Carmo** with its twin towers. It was completed in 1877. The amount of baroque ornamentation inside is overwhelming. The main and side altars are probably 90 percent gold, reflecting the former wealth of the order. The very best wood-carvers were employed here, and the whole is one of the finest examples of *talha dourada* work anywhere in Portugal. There is a cemetery behind the church, and also an interesting ossuary, the ★ **Capela dos Ossos ⑬**, filled with bones, skulls and even human hair.

23

Characteristic facade

Capela dos Ossos

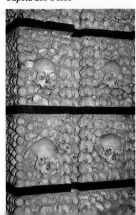

Café in the Jardim Manuel Bivar

A shady place to stop

In the Museu Maritimo

The inscription over the door proclaims 'We Await Thee!'.

For the walk back to the starting-point of the tour, choose one of the narrow picturesque streets such as the Rua da Madalena, the Rua do Compromisso or the Rua Conselheiro Bivar. These small back streets are memorable for their traditional architecture and atmosphere.

The cobbled streets between the typical white houses are very narrow and reserved for pedestrians. It is therefore possible to walk directly to the **Jardim Manuel Bivar** ⑭ with its palm trees and fine cafés. The harbour basin nearby is attractive: rowing boats and pedal boats are still moored there. The Café Aliança, one of the oldest coffee houses in Europe, is on the corner of Rua Francisco Gomes and is a great place for a brief stop – assuming all the seats aren't taken, that is. Even though it's not what it used to be, and the service is slow, the café is still as popular as ever.

Be back at the harbour in time to visit the ★★ **Museu Maritimo Almirante Ramalho Ortigáo** ⑮ (Monday to Friday 9am–12.30pm and 2–5.30pm), tucked away in a corner of the harbourmaster's office (Capitania do Porto de Faro) right beside the 'Eva' hotel. Here you can learn almost everything there is to know about catching fish. There are several old ships: some are of the original size and some are models, e.g. of Vasco da Gama's ship the *São Gabriel*. The exhibits showing the complex way in which the nets are cast underwater are particularly interesting: the methods vary for tuna and for sardines.

Several interesting implements are on display, for example the baskets used for catching lobster or crayfish. The small, waist-high cabinets are treasure troves: each tiny drawer is filled with shells of innumerable kinds, some of incredible shapes and colours – and you're allowed to touch them.

Route 2

The Far End of Europe

Lagos – Ponta da Piedade – Sagres – Cabo de São Vicente (40km/24 miles)

The road to Lagos is lined with the frothy pink blooms of innumerable oleanders. The town shows itself to best advantage the moment you arrive. The new yachting marina gives the place a spirit of adventure. The harbour promenade with its palm trees is very reminiscent of the South of France, and the small bobbing boats are extremely picturesque. This town has a real flair of its own – but it's not its urban qualities that make it special. Lagos's biggest attraction is the large number of sandy bays extending as far as Sagres – and also the weird rock formations on the Ponta da Piedade. Here, where the Atlantic Ocean meets the westernmost point of Europe, nature presents itself in a chromatic symphony: mustard-coloured rocky coastline, deep blue sea, honey-yellow bays and terracotta-brown earth.

In the direction of the Cabo de São Vicente, the vegetation reflects the harsh surroundings. It becomes more sparse, and the trees start looking very weatherbeaten. The steep coast rises to heights of 60m (200ft) or more above

A day in Lagos

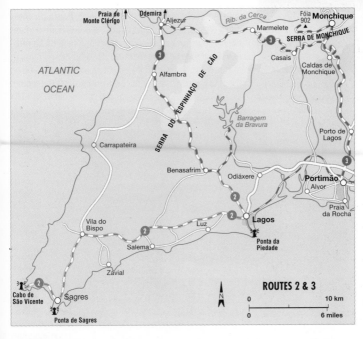

ROUTES 2 & 3

the Atlantic, and sometimes the wind whips the waves right up to the top. The sandy bays are ideal places to sunbathe, and if you take a boat trip through the various grottoes and caves you'll experience the bizarre-looking rock formations at close quarters.

Lagos

It's hard to tell from looking at it, but ★★ **Lagos** is one of the oldest towns in the Algarve as well as one of the most historically interesting. Phoenicians, Greeks and Carthaginians all used this strategically favourable location for commerce between Europe and Africa, and the Romans turned Lacobriga into a flourishing trading centre. In the 8th century the town was captured by sheikhs and caliphs, was fortified with walls and towers, and renamed Zawaia. It became an impregnable fortress and remained so until the 12th century, when the Portuguese kings gradually succeeded in fighting their way to the south coast during the *Reconquista*. The town wall was destroyed during the battles and had to be rebuilt; the wall that surrounds most of the town centre today dates from the 16th century. Despite Lagos's vivid history, little historic substance remains today. Like Faro, much of it was destroyed in the great earthquakes.

If you walk along the promenade to the end of Avenida dos Desobrimentos (Discoveries Avenue), it is a bit like walking back into history: the fort of ★ **Ponta da Bandeira** dates from the 17th century, and was built to guard the harbour from attack. The adjacent **Praça da Republica** lies at the very heart of the town. A bronze monument to Henry the Navigator (*see page 13*), unveiled in 1960 on the 500th anniversary of his death, dominates the square. The prince is holding a sextant and gazing out to sea. His

Lagos's 16th-century wall

Fort Ponta da Bandeira and a nearby beach

head is based on the famous polyptych by the 15th-century painter Vasco Gonçalves, which can be admired in the Museu de Arte Antiga in Lisbon. Lagos has Henry the Navigator to thank for its heyday. He turned the town into a base for the many voyages of discovery that made Portugal so historically important. Lagos was of great strategic importance in Prince Henry's plans.

Wherever you go in this town, words like *Infante, Dom Henrique, Navegador* and *Descobridor* follow you every step of the way. As the governor of Algarve province, Henry resided in the Castelo dos Governadores on the western side of the square. Buried in the ★ **Igreja de Santa Maria** under a magnificent carved altar at the northwestern end, his remains were later transferred to Batalha.

Lagos Marina

Lagos was also the birthplace of Gil Eanes, the discoverer who first sailed around the Cabo Bojador and put an end to the ominous theory that the world ended at the north coast of Africa. The cape had until then been considered unnavigable. Lagos has provided Eanes with only a modest memorial, in spite of the bravery he displayed: it is south of the Praça da Republica and easily missed. Perhaps there are no grand memorials to Eanes because his discovery opened up one of the darkest chapters in Portuguese history: very soon after his voyage Lagos became the first and largest slave market in Europe. Eanes's colleague Antáo Gonçalves brought the first captured Africans here from Senegal in 1441. Those unfortunates who came later were tied to the large iron post under the still-existing arcade of the old custom house, and then auctioned off to the highest bidder.

A few metres away from the Praça, the Rua de S Gonçalo leads off to Lagos's pride and joy, the ★★ **Igreja de Santo Antonio**. The baroque splendour within is scarcely evident from the outside, and the facade is actually quite nondescript. On the other side of the portal, however, is the world of Portuguese *talha dourada*, and for sheer profusion this church cannot be beaten by any others in the Algarve. This single-aisled hall church is quite stunning. Wherever the lavish gilt decoration is absent, blue tiles have been added, and the blue and gold harmonise magnificently. The church was built in 1769 above the ruins of the original structure which was destroyed in the earthquake.

Inside Igreja de Santo Antonio

In a side street by the church – the Rua General Alberto Carlos Silveira – don't miss the ★★ **Museu Municipal de José Formosinho** (Tuesday to Saturday 9.30am–12.30pm and 2–5pm). Alongside several archaeological exhibits, religious artefacts and a few paintings by contemporary artists, there's a charming department devoted to everyday Algarve artefacts. By contrast, the 'deformed animals conserved in spirit' section is rather creepy.

Dona Ana near Lagos

Cut Loose

The rocky coastline is part of the region's appeal

The traffic-free Rua Silva Lopes and Rua 25 de Abril lead directly to the **Praça Gil Eanes**, the liveliest space in town. At the centre stands a statue of King Sebastian (1973) which many people have criticised on the grounds that it is too modern for its subject matter.

It was on 24 June 1578 that the young King Sebastian's armada set sail with 800 ships, 15,000 men and 2,500 cavalrymen in order to force the Moors in Northern Africa to accept Christianity. The foolish and arrogant 24-year-old king refused to take advice or plan for anything but success. In Morocco he drove his men straight into an army five times larger than his own and disappeared under mysterious circumstances. Just 70 of the 17,500 soldiers made it home again.

This disaster resulted in Portugal's dependence on Spain from 1580 onwards, and it only managed to regain its independence in 1640. By then the country had lost much of its international importance. But there has been one long-lasting benefit to the town from King Sebastian's time. In 1576, shortly before he left on his ill-fated crusade, he made Lagos the capital of Algarve.

North of the Praça Gil Eanes stands the **Igreja de São Sebastião**, with its fine Renaissance portal dating from 1530 and three-aisled interior.

Lagos is very lively. It has a population of around 15,000, and this former fishing village has now grown into one of the larger towns of the Algarve. The bizarre rocky coastline and the beautiful beaches have generated a considerable amount of tourism, which has absorbed many of the job losses that occurred when the fishing industry went into decline. The old centre of the town has been revitalised: it is one big pedestrian precinct now, and a very pleasant place for a stroll.

The local beach at Lagos is the **Praia Porto de Mos e Canavial**, and it is broad, flat and ideal for children. The more typical bays you are likely to see in picture postcards can be found along what is known as the Lagos Gold Coast, at beaches like **Camilo**, **Dona Ana** and **Homens-Pinhão**. The longest sandy beach (4km/2½ miles) is the **Meia Praia**. Sports equipment is available for hire practically everywhere.

The main attraction at Lagos is, however, the very strange-looking rock formation south of the town known as the ★★ **Ponta da Piedade**. It has been formed by sea and wind erosion and is unique in Europe. Many of the formations have local nicknames such as 'the kitchen' or the easily visualised ' lady's shoe'. Those interested in taking a boat trip through the grottoes and beneath the cliffs should go down the 200 steps leading to the bay below, where boats await custom.

Leave Lagos in the direction of Vila do Bispo and Sagres along the newly-built, EU-financed motorway. Those keen on ceramics should definitely take the first exit. The road carries on parallel to the motorway for a while before heading off inland, to the ceramic workshop of the artists Jorge Mealha and Jeanette Brown. Here you can have your own – not entirely cheap – clay collector's item produced before your very eyes. The workshop takes a bit of finding, and is called Casa dos Oleiros.

Roughly 7km (4 miles) along the motorway outside Lagos is the town of **Almadena**, which has a very good restaurant, O Poço (*see page 65*). A little further on, **Vila do Bispo** is the main town in the region, but with its population of just 1,700 it is also the smallest town in all of the Algarve, and a very sleepy little place indeed. The Igreja Matriz is very pretty, with its fine 18th-century tiles and *talha dourada*.

The next town on the route is ★★ **Sagres** (pop. 2,300), an historic town and a magnet for the tourists. The population here has doubled over the last 10 years, but apart

On and in Villa do Infante

29

from the crush of tourist buses up at the *fortaleza* of Henry the Navigator, there's no more happening here today than there was before. Even the brewery that makes the famous *Sagres* beer will be sought in vain – it is located near Lisbon, and it only uses the name because of its historical connotations. Sagres is closely bound up with the phase of great discoveries ushered in by Henry the Navigator.

High up on a rocky outcrop above the sea are the remains of a fortress, the ★ **Vila do Infante**, in which Henry the Navigator is said to have planned the great voyages. The complex standing today dates from the 16th century, and was greatly altered after the great earthquake of 1755.

Tackling the daily tasks

At the centre is the tiny **Capela Nossa Senhora da Graça**; Henry may have prayed in its predecessor. Outside the chapel an enormous wind rose is laid out in stones. Overgrown with weeds, the *Rosa dos Ventos* is 43m (141ft) across. For a long time it was the most visible proof of the scientific importance of this site. The division into 42 sections is unusual: most wind roses have 32.

Rosa dos Ventos

Very little remains of the great era of Henry the Navigator and his 'school'. The fortress is presently an enormous construction site, and the youth hostel is closed. The old building, constructed according to plans dating from the 16th century, has been bulldozed – nobody knows exactly why – and the new building in the centre of the fortified complex is looking increasingly box-like, a modern disaster.

The nearby bays and sandy beaches are attractive to look at, but the Atlantic climate on the west coast is harsh and there is usually quite a fierce wind blowing. The water here is also a lot colder than on the beaches further east. The Praia de Beliche is 5km (3 miles) from Sagres, 500m (1,600ft) long, free of rocks, and a popular meeting point for anglers. The Praia de Tonel in the next bay has superb underwater scenery and is ideal for diving or snorkelling. A little further west are the Praia de Mareta – whose shallow waters make it particularly suitable for children – and the Praia Baleeira. The Praia Martinhal, 2km (1 mile) north of Sagres, is distinctive for its large sand dunes and is an ideal starting-point for windsurfers.

Europe comes to an end at the ★★ **Cabo de São Vicente**, the southwesternmost point of Portugal and the entire continent. The lighthouse on top, 60m (200ft) above the Atlantic Ocean, and the cliffs all around provide a spectacular view. Try to come here in the evening if possible, after all the tourist buses have left. The place is really peaceful then, and the sunsets are often spectacular. Fishermen in the Middle Ages, and many seafarers, believed this was where the world ended: *o Fim do Mundo*.

At Cabo de São Vicente

The **lighthouse** has been here since 1846, and its lens is the largest in Europe at 2.66m (9ft) in diameter. The beam of light can reach 90km (48.6 nautical miles) across the sea. Even though most ships today are equipped with radar and other devices, these lighthouses are still very useful for orientation purposes. Officially the tower can't be visited, though sometimes the friendly lighthouse keepers (*faroleiros*) will allow tour guides with groups to look around. The view from the top is stunning. Don't touch the glass, though – the *faroleiros* are proud of keeping it absolutely spotless. Every fingerprint is removed with a cloth instantly.

Route 3

*Restaurant in the
Serra de Monchique*

31

PORTUGAL

Algarve

Faro

One Hundred Years of Solitude

**Lagos – Aljezur – Serra de Monchique – Monchique
– Caldas de Monchique (92km/57 miles)**

The **Serra de Monchique** forms a highly impressive contrast to the Atlantic coast. Eucalyptus, pine, cork oak and olives grow high up on the mountainside, and these regions alternate with others of sudden aridity, with gorse, rosemary and scrubland. Fertile valleys lie between these contrasting landscapes, sometimes irrigated by rivers – if they haven't dried up. The harsh, rocky landscape and the windy coast in the west have been quite an obstacle to tourism so far.

Aljezur is the first relatively large town on the route from Lagos. Then, further eastwards, Monchique appears. Apart from these two towns the entire Serra is practically uninhabited. The rhythm of nature determines the lives and work of the farmers and fishermen. Time seems to stand still in the remote mountain villages. One hundred years of solitude – and the region is still neglected today. The roads are bumpy and full of potholes, and one gets the distinct impression that money from the EU is not being used to improve conditions here. The locals have used what new roads there are to leave the region as fast as they can. There are numerous deserted farmhouses, many of them totally dilapidated. Those who still live here have come to terms with their harsh existence, so you can still find what is often called 'picturesque' – a mixture of poverty and archaic tradition.

A word of warning: in July and August forest fires are a permanent menace. Before you travel, ask at a tourist office or your hotel about the current state of affairs.

Mule riding

Aljezur's Castelo

Enjoying the views

The road that leads northwards from Lagos deteriorates from Bensafrim onwards, becoming bumpy and narrow. The scenery makes up for it, though: there are several magnificent avenues of fir and pine. They will probably be chopped down, however, if the government receives the money it has been promised for highway construction. As you approach **Aljezur** (pop. 3,500), just before the border with the Alentejo, the Moorish castle can be seen from afar, high up on its hill, around which the white houses of the small town are clustered. The Castelo, which was captured from the Moors in 1246 by soldiers of the Order of Santiago, is in ruins, but the view from the top is still magnificent.

Although it is separated from Aljezur by fields and a river, **Igreja Nova** still belongs to the town, though today it has outgrown its parent. Agriculture is still very important here: men and women can be seen bending down among melons, maize, potatoes and onions. They still use the old hoe known as the *enxada* to till the soil, and mules can often be seen standing around in the hot sun, waiting patiently. The beaches here can only be reached by car, along several hairpin bends up the cliffs and then down the other side again. Parking places are rare. The small Praia de Monte Clérigo is 5km (3 miles) from Aljezur, and the Praia das Amoreiras 7km (4 miles). The water is ice-cold, however. Beware of the *peixe aranha*, too: it's a fish with poisonous spines that digs itself into shallow areas and doesn't like being trodden on.

In Igreja Nova the road leading to Monchique branches off to the right. Soon the agricultural region is far behind, and the once heavily forested **★★ Serra de Monchique**, today covered with eucalyptus trees, comes into view. The tree, which smells so good and forms the basis for wonderful essences, also destroys the soil and is very flammable. With its broad and arid areas, the region still hasn't recovered from the fires of the past years. Shallow-rooted trees like the pine are completely destroyed, but deep-rooted trees like the eucalyptus tend to recover quite quickly. Arsonists have also been at work in this area, not least to serve the interests of the timber industry, but the fires are also due to insufficient care of the forests. On one weekend in August the fire brigade were fighting blazes at 1,500 different locations. What little remains of the Serra de Monchique's original trees and vegetation is rather depressing. There used to be a very unusual and exotic mixture of pine, chestnut, cork oak, walnut, banana and strawberry tree here. Even though most of them have now disappeared, the spring colours created in some regions by a variety of other plants – magnolia, heather, oleander, rhododendron and rosemary – are still very impressive.

Just before you arrive in Monchique, **Meia Vana** is a good place to buy traditional craftwork. Senhor Carlos has nearly everything that's typical of the mountain regions inside his Casa do Gato: thick woollen pullovers, attractive folding chairs made of walnut, sheepskins, wild-heather honey (*mel de urze*), pure eucalyptus oil, and *medronho* spirit, distilled from the fruit of the strawberry tree, which can be sampled on the premises. *Serranos* (mountain dwellers) like drinking their *medronho* sweetened with a little local honey.

Monchique

Manueline portal

The mountain village of ★ **Monchique** was practically unknown before it received its royal visit in 1495: the ailing King João II came here to take the mountain air on the advice of his personal physician. Since then the population has swelled to 5,200, but the whole place is still very much a village.

In the main square, the Largo 5 de Outubro, is the A Nora café – a good place to wind down and relax. Portuguese men and travellers sit on the terrace here, but hardly ever any Portuguese women: they don't go to cafés, that's always been the rule here. Most of the visitors here just come for the day, usually in their own cars; they drive up to the highest point in the Algarve, the Fóia (902m/ 2,960ft), and then vanish again in the direction of the coast. This is a pity, because this region is ideal for hiking – though no maps are available.

By the way, don't miss a visit to the ★ **Igreja Matriz**, Monchique's parish church, with its impressive Manueline portal. A rope motif hewn from the stone encloses a kind of oriental headdress. This relic of Portuguese naval expansion looks very out of place these days. Another sight

33

Igreja Matriz interior

The ruined Convento

worth seeing is the dilapidated Franciscan ★ **Convento da Nossa Senhora do Desterro**, built in 1632. The coat of arms on the facade commemorates Dom Pedro da Silvas, the founder of the convent and later viceroy of India. A short distance below is the attractively tiled fountain known as the Fonte dos Passarinhos – with an impressive magnolia next to it.

The road leads past terraces to the 902-m (2,960-ft) high peak of **Fóia**. It is badly disfigured by radio masts, but if you turn your back on them the view from the top is magnificent, with Faro visible on clear days. If it's a very warm day there will be a heat haze.

A doorway in Caldas de Monchique

The nostalgic spa town of ★★ **Caldas de Monchique** is 6km (3 miles) south of Monchique. Its sulphur springs were famous in Roman times and are supposed to cure rheumatism, skin diseases and digestive problems. Just two drops of the water, rumour has it, can prolong your life by several years – one reason King João II (1481–95) came here to take the waters. The climate and the water didn't do him much good, however. He died aged 40 in Alvor after his rest-cure at Caldas de Monchique. He never lived to hear of the success of his last great project: the discovery of the sea route to India by Vasco da Gama.

Sampling the water

The spa at Caldas flourished around the turn of the century, when it became an extremely fashionable place for the nobility to take the waters. Several attractive art nouveau facades still date from that time. From then on, however, the town was gradually forgotten. Today it's a sleepy place, but gradually growing more lively thanks to tourism. If you'd like to try the waters here for free, go inside the small, Moorish-style annexe to the old spa building, where the water comes straight out of the wall.

Route 4

The Gold Coast

Alvor – Praia da Rocha – Portimão – Ferragudo – Silves – Albufeira (55km/34 miles)

Very little of the famous Gold Coast is unspoilt by tourist development. The holiday ghettoes, built with no consideration for landscape, have little to do with Portugal. Alvor and Ferragudo are not quite as touristy, and nor is sleepy Silves up in the mountains. The classic features of Algarve advertising – colourful fishing boats and almond blossom – are still around, but only because they help boost the region's image. Hardly anyone fishes for a living any more. Mass tourism hit the stretch between Praia da Rocha and Albufeira particularly hard, and not without reason: there are miles of sandy beach here, set against a magnificent backdrop of deep-blue sea and golden rock. If you can ignore the high-rise hotels and crowds, Praia da Rocha has very impressive natural rock formations. There's a lot going on in Portimão, a centre of the fishing industry, but the town itself has little charm. Shopping is very good, however, and entertainment through the night is no problem either. Try the grilled sardines at the harbour – they're delicious.

Praia da Rocha

35

Boat for hire at Portimão

The old road to **Alvor** (pop. 7,000), paved with granite, was built 20 years ago but is still in good condition. An asphalt road would have been destroyed by the hot sun long ago. Although it's not right on the coast, Alvor, with its labyrinth of alleyways and numerous cafés, is one of the more pleasant towns of the region. Don't look for any historic architecture, however – the 1755 earthquake destroyed the town totally. Despite that, one of the finest churches in Southern Portugal is here: the ★ **Igreja Matriz**. The Manueline portal with its various nautical mo-

High-rise rocks at Praia da Rocha

tifs will delight photographers, and the mighty red columns inside, made of Silves stone, are also most impressive. Needless to say there is also some magnificent *talha dourada* to be admired here, as well as some polychromatic tile decoration dating from the 18th century. The portal is the only historic sight, and it dates from the period when Portugal had risen to become a leading colonial power. Five hundred years later, Alvor was host to the signing of a treaty that ended Portugal's colonial power: the Treaty of Alvor (1975) was designed to remove the threat of civil war in newly independent Angola and help the country form a new government.

Around 50 years ago the neighbouring town of ★ **Praia da Rocha**, 4km (2½ miles) further eastwards, was an idyllic little resort. Today the place is more reminiscent of Manhattan than anything else. The whole sea promenade (Avenida Tomas Cabreira) is lined by high-rise hotels, restaurants, fast-food outlets, ice-cream parlours, bars, souvenir shops, travel agencies and rental car firms – everything a tourist could need. The green of vegetation is rare among all the grey concrete. It's no consolation to know that Portugal's former president, Mario Soares, stays at his summer house here every year. The town's most important – and only – asset is its unusual rocky beach, which should definitely be seen. If you can close your eyes to the threatening concrete jungle, even the sandy beach isn't that bad: it is about 1 mile (1.6km) long, and contrasts spectacularly with the weird rock shapes, which have names such as *Três Ursus* (three bears), *Três Irmáos* (three brothers) and *Arco de Triunfo* (triumphal arch). Geologists are worried that this stretch of rocky coastline won't last much longer – the forces of natural erosion cannot be halted.

On the beach

It's hard to get any sleep in Praia da Rocha. The discos rarely close before three or four in the morning, and at around 6am the refuse collectors start their rounds. As far as sunbathing is concerned: if the beach at Praia da Rocha is too full, two alternatives are the Praia dos Três Irmãos, or Alvor. Water sports enthusiasts will find equipment for hire at both beaches for surfing, sailing, waterskiing and snorkelling.

The town of **Portimão** (pop. 34,000), 7km (4 miles) further west, is not very popular despite its size. It is a hectic, busy place, with little that is picturesque. Most tourists come here to buy souvenirs or stock their fridges. It used to be a Roman harbour called Portus Magnus at the delta of the Arade river. During the Moorish occupation the town was overshadowed by the Algarve capital of Silves, until the Arade silted up and Silves' fortunes waned when the boats couldn't sail that far up river. From the 19th century onwards Portimão grew to become one of the most important fishing towns of Portugal. The first canned sardine factory was opened here in 1891, and the town was the centre of the Algarve fish-canning industry for decades. The disused ★ **fishing harbour** still smells of tar, diesel and fish. It was replaced by a more modern harbour in 1991, but a few sardine fishermen still set out from here and bring their delicious catch back to be grilled. Today, however, tourism is the main source of income.

Portimão church

37

One of the last genuine fishing villages in western Algarve is ★★ **Ferragudo**. Despite the relentless construction all around, this place has preserved its special character, and most of its 1,911 inhabitants still earn a living fishing. It sits picturesquely in a bay opposite Portimão. The cobbled streets are largely deserted at noon, the colourful fishing boats bob at anchor, and there are fishing nets and a few rusty anchors at the quayside. In the evenings the odd fisherman – often with beret and cigarette – can be seen mending his nets. The women place the catch out to dry. Ferragudo is a beautiful place.

Ferragudo's beach

In contrast, the ambitious regional centre of **Lagoa** (pop. 5,000) is not that appealing, though the landscape is an attractive mixture of red earth and green vines. This place goes crazy once a year, during the wine harvest in late August and early September, when innumerable mule- and donkey-drawn carts arrive here – the local farmers bringing their wine to be pressed. The wine can be purchased direct from the vintners at the turn-off to Carvoeiro.

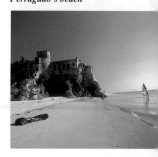

Carvoeiro also has a good beach: small but pretty and in the middle of a luxury tourist complex. The other local beaches – Vale de Centianes, Barranquinho, Alban-

Silves Castelo

deira and Marinha – are all jammed between cliffs and steep rocks. Sometimes 160 steps or more have to be descended to reach a beach. Out of season they're pleasantly deserted, as are the numerous beach bars and restaurants.

The town of ★★ **Silves** is to the north of Lagoa. Drive about 500 yards/metres into town in the direction of Faro to an observation point that provides the best view of the town's skyline. On top of the hill is the gigantic Moorish castle, and to the left is the white cathedral which the Christians built on the ruins of a mosque.

Silves, known to the Arabs as Xelb, was a flourishing trade centre when it became the Moorish capital of Algarve. There were more than 20 mosques in the town, and the harbour on the Rio Arade was enormous for that time. Silves was on a par with Granada and Cordoba, the other Moorish capitals on the Iberian Peninsula, in economic prowess and cultural prestige. It was far larger and wealthier than Lisbon, with a population of around 30,000 – three times as many people as today. It was only in 1242 that King Afonso III finally managed to capture this well fortified Moorish city.

The ★★ **Castelo**, restored in 1940, once had two sets of battlemented walls, underground storerooms and two cisterns that annually collected enough water to last one year – thus making it virtually impregnable. Walk around the outer wall and enjoy the fascinating views. The experience is particularly memorable in almond-blossom time, and also in July when the oranges and lemons are ripening. The valleys around Silves grow the best citrus fruit in Portugal.

As the Rio Arade gradually silted up, the city lost its importance. These days, not much remains of its former magnificence – the 1755 earthquake spared very few buildings. The Gothic ★ **Cathedral** was built between the 13th and 15th centuries and is considered one of the most important religious structures in the Algarve. The main facade is flanked by two bell-towers; the left has a Gothic window, the right one a clock. The church as it looks today was built during baroque times: the inscription above the main portal reads 1781.

Silves' Gothic Cathedral

Ponte Romana

Also impressive is the ★ **Ponte Romana**. The seven-arched bridge is considered Roman, but is more probably 13th century, possibly built on the ruins of a previous Roman structure. Its construction is a masterpiece of masonry. At the eastern edge of the town is a 3-m (11-ft) high Manueline cross dating from the early 16th century, the *Cruz de Portugal*. Made of white limestone, it is finely sculpted on both sides and shows various scenes from the Passion. The ★ **Museu Municipal de Arqueologia** (14 Rua das Portas de Loulé, daily except Sunday and pub-

lic holidays 10am–12.30pm and 2.30–6pm) has exhibits dating from prehistoric times to the 17th century. The highlight is a 900-year-old Arab fountain, discovered during excavations in 1979, around which the museum was built.

Albufeira, the 'white town by the blue sea'

39

'The white town by the blue sea,' **Albufeira** was once fondly called. The small fishing village of Roman and Moorish origins used to sit on the clifftop on the site of a Moorish fortress. Gradually the inhabitants moved further down the hill as far as the bay and the beach. The various layers of the town can be viewed best from the ★ **Miradouro do Patio**.

The sun sets on the praia

When the earthquake struck in 1755, the town was hit by a massive tidal wave. Scarcely 30 houses were left standing. Nevertheless, the ★ **Cidade Velha** (Old Town) still looks centuries-old. Albufeira has retained all the charms of the fishing village it once was. On the ★ **Praia dos Pescadores** there are still numerous gaily-coloured fishing boats – and they're not just decorative. The whiff of sardines in the air makes it clear that fishing is still very much a part of local life.

A second Albufeira has grown up around the old centre. It is the largest holiday resort in the Algarve: modern, noisy, and geared completely to the demands of the tourist trade. In July and August the town's 26,000 inhabitants are definitely in the minority. Winter is the only time things get any quieter here.

The best beaches in the area of Albufeira have superb rocky coastal scenery, and include Praia da Galé, Castelo, Balbinas and São Rafael, and are easily accessible by car. The Praia de Baleeira lies at the foot of Albufeira. The Praia de Oura is famous for its new Atlantic Diving Centre, and the long sandy Praia de Falesia, which extends as far as Vilamoura, is a special favourite with windsurfers and yachtsmen alike.

Taking the plunge near Albufeira

Vilamoura rooftop

Route 5

Blue Sea and Bare Mountains

Albufeira – Paderne – Alte – Salir – Querença – Loulé – Almancil – Vilamoura (79km/49 miles)

The landscape north of Albufeira marks the transition from the Serra de Monchique to the Serra do Caldeirão, and it is full of striking contrasts: blue sea, arid hill scenery, yellow cornfields, fruit groves and vineyards. It is hilly but not mountainous. The *Algarvios* have their own name for the region: the *barrocal*. The villages here – Paderne, Alte, Salir and Querença – have a special charm of their own. They stand out like tiny jewels against the rough hill scenery, small ensembles of white and graceful houses, overgrown with jacaranda and bougainvillea. The rural architecture here is very famous, especially the elaborately decorated chimneys on the houses. Tourists hardly ever go to the *barrocal*, even in high season, because of the poor roads. The only village they visit regularly is Alte, because it is part of several tour programmes.

The vegetation in this region is varied, with carobs, almonds, figs and olives growing along the steep slopes. The *barrocal* is nearest to what the Algarve used to look like. Anyone intending to visit the magnificent church in Almancil should start their return journey to the coast before 7pm, before the gates close. Vilamoura is ideal for night-owls and those interested in Roman mosaics.

As soon as you leave the N125 things get quieter and the bustle of coastal life gradually dies away. Rock roses, thistles and scrub protect the ground from the scorching sun. All kinds of geckoes and lizards – and sometimes the odd chameleon – live in this undergrowth. Things get greener again near the mountain village of ★ **Paderne** (pop. 2,800), northwest of Albufeira. Paderne supplies Portugal with its best peaches and apricots. The ruined castle and a Gothic church are the most striking buildings in this idyllic village with its narrow winding streets.

The road passes various species of tree: oak, orange, olive and also carob or *alfarrobeiras*. Carobs are tall, with gnarled trunks and an evergreen canopy of leaves – just the thing for a hot day. The long seed-pods called *alfarrobas* that dangle from these trees each June once provided nourishment for poor farmers. The fruit is rich in protein and is used to bake bread. A nutritious brown mass resembling chocolate is also produced from it. There is a carob processing centre just above Paderne. This multipurpose fruit is used by the animal food, textile, leather, cosmetic and pharmaceutical industries.

Peaceful Paderne

Being taken for a ride

Near Portela de Messines the route continues east into the ★ **Serra do Caldeirão**, a brownish-green hilly district with many valleys. After passing a lot of fig and orange trees, you'll arrive at the most picturesque village in the region: ★★ **Alte**, right at the centre of the Serra do Caldeirão. Alte came second in a 'most typically Por-

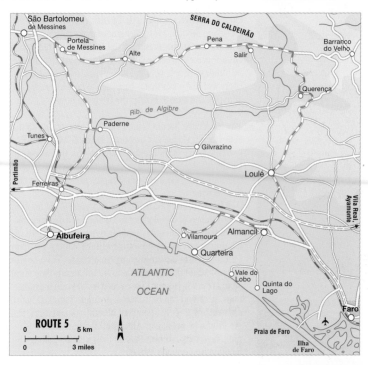

A symbol of wealth

In a country garden

tuguese village' competition organised under Salazar in 1938, but national acknowledgement was slow in coming back then. Today tourists come here in busloads.

It's best to park your car at the entrance to the village and walk the rest of the way on foot. The streets get narrower and narrower, and what little space there is for parking has already been taken by the local residents – the pretty little village has a population of 2,400. Alte is a good place to stroll through. The cobblestones, worn smooth by the footsteps of so many visitors, glint in the sunlight. The walls of the houses are all freshly whitewashed, and high on their roofs you can see the decorative *chaminés*, the pride of every Algarve house. These chimneys come in all shapes and sizes and are counted among the finest in the region. A chimney was formerly a symbol of wealth. Everywhere the whitewash is livened up by the odd splash of bright natural colour from oleander, bougainvillea, jacaranda and pomegranate trees. Dangling in many of the windows are birdcages containing songbirds. Not many of the birds sing: it is a strange and common hobby in Portugal to catch wild birds and lock them in cages.

At the centre of the village, the ★ **Igreja de Nossa Senhora de Assunção** is a real jewel. Like most churches it's almost always locked, but the Manueline portal on the outside makes up for that. A little further on is the small **Capela de Nossa Senhora de Lurdes**, decorated with rare tiles from Seville. Most Portuguese make pilgrimages to Alte for the **springs,** and for the waterfall called Fonte Grande at the exit of the village. At weekends and on public holidays people wait in long queues to fill plastic canisters with the water that is supposed to cure all manner of ailments and banish evil spirits from the home.

The landscape becomes hillier now. The terraces on the ever steeper slopes are supported by small walls of slate – the typical construction material of the Serra do Caldeirão. Now and then you will spot the odd disused windmill along the way, with drooping sails and rather forlorn looking.

Sleepy Salir

After a while ★ **Salir** comes into view – yet another sleepy village at the southern end of the Serra do Caldeirão. From the *castelo* – today nothing more than a few Moorish remains at the centre of the village – there's a magnificent view of the surrounding countryside. This site was once of strategic importance to the Moors in their fight against the Christians. Like everywhere else in the mountains, here you can buy cheese, *presunto* (smoked ham), *chouriço* or *linguiça* (smoked blood/pork sausage), and *medronho* (a schnaps). Almost all the houses in this region have long wooden bars on their kitchen ceilings for hanging home-made sausages.

The scenery looks even more primeval as ★ **Querença** approaches. There are cork oaks and strawberry trees everywhere. The eucalyptus has moved in too. A high, whitewashed wall leads the way into the centre of this mountain village, 276m (905ft) above sea level. The small 16th-century pilgrimage church of **Nossa Senhora da Assunção** here is also the parish church for the 1,800 people in the village. The church was more popular in days gone by because the famous pilgrimage route to Santiago de Compostela used to come this way. Its portal is decorated with unusually simple Manueline ornaments. Directly opposite is the Café D Rosa, a good place to take a break and sample the excellent fig or almond cake. On the other side of the village the landscape is less hilly, with extensive plots of almond, fig, olive and carob.

Loulé's lively market

In the direction of ★★ **Loulé** (pop. 20,000) the quality of the road improves. The largest inland town in the Algarve and the economic centre of the area, Loulé holds a market every Saturday that attracts enormous crowds. In the neo-Moorish ★★ **market halls** with their pink-coloured onion domes on the Largo Gago Coutinho tables are loaded to overflowing with an amazing assortment of locally grown fruits and vegetables. It's all ripe, freshly harvested, and tastes delicious. There's also seafood and meat on sale – plus live chickens and rabbits, herbs, potatoes, olives, beans, you name it. People who can't find enough room to spread their wares indoors come out and lay them on the ground instead.

The neo-Moorish market halls

The Moors left Portugal a long time ago, but this place is very reminiscent of Morocco. The main shopping streets – Praça da Republica and Rua 5 de Outubro – mostly sell shoes and craftware. As you walk, note the pavement: it's covered with ornamental patterns in white limestone and black basalt by *calceteiros* (mosaicists). This craft, for

43

Interior detail,
Nossa Senhorada Conceição

Leather worker

which Portugal has long been famed, is gradually dying out. Not far from the Largo Bernardo Lopes are the remains of the *castelo* – which was probably Moorish in origin – and the old town wall. The houses here are so crowded together that the castle is quite easy to miss.

The small pilgrimage chapel of ★ **Nossa Senhora da Conceição** opposite the tourist information centre has a very unassuming facade but contains fine *azulejo* decoration and also a valuable *talha* altar. The tiles are 17th-century and show scenes from *The Life of the Virgin*.

The Largo Dom Pedro I leads straight to the old town, ★ **Almedina**, traditionally inhabited by craftsmen since Moorish times. These days Loulé's industrial production of craft goods has thinned down their numbers somewhat, and the saddlers who used to make the decorative reins for donkey carts are as good as unemployed. The **Igreja Matriz** on the Largo Cabrita de Silva contains some fine *azulejos* tile decoration. The Gothic structure dates from the 13th century and contains some impressive columns and Renaissance altars. Two streets further on, the ★ **Igreja da Misericordia** in the Avenida Duarte Pacheco has a magnificent Manueline portal that demonstrates Loulé's importance during the era of great discoveries. The town is also famed for its many original chimneys and for the carnival that takes place here in the four days preceding Ash Wednesday.

The village of **Almancil** has a very special sight: up on a hill above the pretty *casas algarvias* is the originally Romanesque ★★ **Igreja de São Lourenço de Matos** (Tuesday to Saturday 10am–1pm and 2.30–7pm), a tiny church decorated inside right up to its dome with magnificent blue *azulejos* tiles. Made in 1730 by Policarpo de Oliveira Bernardes, they depict *The Martyrdom of St Laurence* in

Igreja de São Lourenço de Matos

the 3rd century. The fathers of the church had him roasted over a glowing griddle for distributing among the poor money that should have been spent on building churches. It is said that halfway through this gruesome execution he shouted out sarcastically to the priests that he wasn't quite done enough on one side. The tiles, the marble altar and the *talha dourada* at São Lourenço make the little church a masterpiece of architectural unity. Beneath the church is the **Centro Cultural de São Lourenço**. It has interesting exhibitions and concerts and also a theatre and a cinema.

★ **Vilamoura** is the largest private holiday complex in the Algarve. Planned in the 1960s, it is still considered a masterpiece of all that is luxurious and gigantic. At the heart of Vilamoura is a yachting marina: with 1,000 berths it is one of the largest and most modern in Europe, almost as large as the marina in St-Tropez. Numerous luxury hotels have sprung up around the marina, along with sports facilities, four of the most famous golf courses on the Iberian Peninsula, and a private airport. The famous luxury holiday resorts of Quinta do Lago, Vila Sol and Vale de Lobo are right next door. This puts Vilamoura right at the top of all the resorts in the Algarve.

When the Portuguese industrialist Cupertino de Miranda began his dream town here in 1963, Vilamoura (Moorish Town) was nothing more than a tiny rural settlement. Beyond the marina there used to be fields, and the archaeologist José Farajota noticed farmers tearing up Roman mosaics as they ploughed the fields. Systematic excavation of the site has continued since 1971, bringing to light ★ **Cerro da Vila** (guided tours Monday to Friday 10.30am and 2pm), extensive ruins dating from the Roman, Visigothic and Arab epochs. An area of 3 hectares (8 acres) has so far been uncovered, but archaeologists believe the site could cover up to 8 hectares (20 acres). The Casa do Mosaicos contains a number of well-preserved Roman mosaics from a former villa along with the remains of a bath-house and some fragments of stucco. To reach the Cerro da Vila, simply follow the signposts to *Estaçáo Arqueologica*.

There is a variety of beaches in the area. The Praia de Vilamoura is a broad sandy beach with red rocky cliffs and good for water sports. Trafal is similar but a lot quieter and difficult to reach. Marinha is well protected and thus ideal for children, and the beaches of Vale do Lobo and Garráo are backed by attractive dunes. The Praia de Ançáo and Praia Quinta do Lago are part of the Ria Formosa nature reserve. Sand predominates here, and further inland there are several pine groves which sometimes result in mosquito problems at the height of summer.

Igreja de São Lourenço de Matos detail

45

The good life in Vilamoura's marina

A secluded corner

PORTUGAL

Algarve

Faro

Route 6

Where East Meets West

Olhão – Ria Formosa – Fuseta – Moncarapacho – Estói – São Brás de Alportel (33km/20 miles)

Ferry from Olhão

Olhão is an intriguing place – is it really still Europe, or is it North Africa? Though distant geographically, North Africa is definitely present architecturally. The narrow streets in the old centre can get crowded rapidly, turning the place into something reminiscent of a Moroccan casbah. Seen from above, the impression is even greater – the Cubism of Braques seems to have become reality. The reddish-gold rocky coast has disappeared, but there are endless beaches. This is the *Sotavento* – the eastern, less tourist-orientated part of the Algarve. The beaches are quieter, and the lagoons of the Ria Formosa have been turned

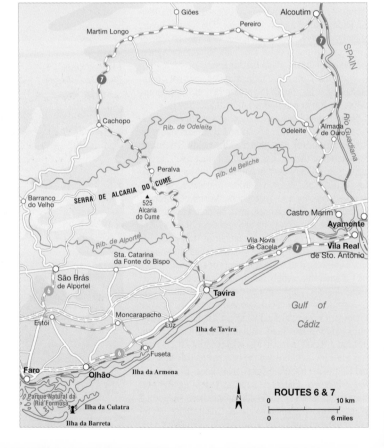

Giões
Pereiro
Alcoutim
Martim Longo
SPAIN
Cachopo
Rib. de Odeleite
Odeleite
Almada de Ouro
Rio Guadiana
Peralva
Rib. de Beliche
Barranco do Velho
SERRA DE ALCARIA DO CUME
▲ 525 Alcaria do Cume
Castro Marim
Ayamonte
Rib. de Alportel
Vila Nova de Cacela
Vila Real de Sto. Antônio
Sta. Catarina da Fonte do Bispo
São Brás de Alportel
Tavira
Estói
Moncarapacho
Luz
Ilha de Tavira
Gulf of Cádiz
Fuseta
Faro
Olhão
Ilha da Armona
Parque Natural da Ria Formosa
Ilha da Culatra
N

ROUTES 6 & 7

0   10 km

0   6 miles

Ilha da Barreta

into a conservation area. If you travel further inland towards Moncarapacho and Estói you will reach fertile landscape again, filled with orange and lemon trees, roses and cork oaks.

Olhão has a North African flavour

With its cube-shaped houses, ★ **Olhão** is the most Moorish-looking Algarve town – even though it was only built in the 18th century, long after the Moors had left the region for good. The fishermen and merchants who used to sail across to the coast of Morocco were only copying what they had seen on the other continent.

Straw goods

47

The architecture of the old town, or ★★ **Barreta**, is strictly geometrical and devoid of ornamentation. The white, two- or three-storey cubic houses stand close together, providing plenty of shade, and creating long facades that are broken only occasionally by small passageways or archways. Steep and narrow staircases – both outdoor and indoor – lead up to the flat roofs, which are surrounded by low walls called *platibandas*, creating geometrical areas (*açoteias*).

The cube-like verandas are connected to one another by flights of steps. On top of the buildings are small towers (*mirantes*), and the typical chimneys – although they are rather less ornate than chimneys elsewhere in the Algarve. In the old days fruit was laid out on the *açoteias* to dry, and in winter the slightly sloping roofs were used to collect rainwater which was then diverted to cisterns. Today the terraces are mainly used for drying washing or as convenient places to put television aerials.

The best place for a view of the roofs of Olhão is from the bell tower of the ★ **Igreja de Nossa Senhora do Rosario** (daily 9am–noon and 4–5.30pm). The forest of television aerials has robbed the scene of some of its charm, however. Be advised: do *not* climb the church tower anywhere near the hour, because the church bells are extremely loud and can make you temporarily deaf. The church was built by the fishermen of Olhão between 1681 and 1698, at their own expense. At the beginning of the 19th century they successfully defended it against the French invaders. However, during the 20th century it remained closed for years on end due to a lack of worshippers. It was not until 1990 that Padre Cunha and Padre Afonso came here to build up a new parish.

The famous square houses of Olhão mean that the town is frequently visited, and as a result it has sacrificed just about all of its natural beauty to tourism. Despite this it has remained a refreshingly natural town in many respects, possibly because, together with Portimão, Olhão is the most important centre of the Algarve fishing industry. This means the town is not so preoccupied with tourists as might otherwise have been the case. Most tourists come here just to look at the architecture and to wander around the picturesque old town. There is nothing here to make them stay for an extra day or two, and so hotels and guest houses are few.

The mercado, inside and out

There is another Olhão attraction worth seeking out, however. The ★★ **Mercado** (market, 7am–2pm) down at the harbour has an oriental flair all of its own. Distinguished by its Arabian towers, the market has two halls that are filled to the brim with vast quantities of fish, vegetables and spices. The whole place is very busy, very noisy, and quite an experience.

Outside the hall you will find row upon row of dog sharks (*caçáo*) hanging out to dry – looking for all the world like coat hangers. On the opposite side of the street are lots of cafés where the men take life easy while their wives do the shopping. If you don't fancy relaxing with the menfolk, the pedestrian precinct around Rua do Comércio is a pleasant place for a shopping stroll.

Shopping in Olhão

The Algarve has an astonishing variety of birdlife. Around 300 species are either native to Southern Portugal or use these regions as a stopover on their way to or from Africa. The birdlife was one of the main reasons behind the foundation of the ★★ **Parque Natural da Ria Formosa** in 1987. The entrance is 4km (2½ miles) to the west of Olhão – follow signs saying *Quinta de Marim*. Covering a total of 17,000 hectares (42,000 acres), this nature reserve stretches for 55km (34 miles) along the coast from Ancão to Cacelha Velha. Many species of fish breed in the lagoons, which also provide an ideal habitat for storks, flamingos, wild geese and eagles, as well as mussels and prawns. The modern information centre contains a detailed map of the reserve, and there is a nature trail. The famous web-footed Portuguese dog known as the *cão d'agua*, which was traditionally used for fishing, is also bred here (*see page 9*).

Parque Natural da Ria Formosa

The beaches of the islands of **Armona** and **Culatra** are right on Olhão's doorstep. From June until September they can be reached by ferry: the ships dock at the fishing harbour, close to the market halls. Both ferries depart every 1–2 hours; the trip to Armona takes 20 minutes, to Culatra 30 minutes. A boat from Fuseta (*see below*) takes beach lovers to Armona half-hourly from July to August.

The neighbouring fishing town of ★ **Fuseta** (pop. 2,500) is a bit like a miniature Olhão. It, too, is famous for its terraces and cubic buildings – but being smaller than its big brother 10km (6 miles) up the coast, it is also more attractive. The best view is from the church. The beach runs along the edge of a lagoon. It has several bars and restaurants and is a very relaxing place.

Moncarapacho

The road inland to Estói will take you through **Moncarapacho** (pop. 5,500), which has some minor Renaissance and baroque buildings. The **Capela Santo Cristo** contains some fine *azulejos* – the trouble is, it's almost always closed. The **Museu Paroquial** (access via the church) has a small exhibition of old amphorae, ceramics and religious art, and also a coin collection. There are several archaeological finds on display in a small, fenced-off square in front of the church.

The sleepy mountain village of ★★ **Estói** has a clock tower showing the right time, but life here can't be measured in minutes or hours. It's hard to believe that the most magnificent building in the Algarve is hidden away behind a wall just a short distance from the church.

The building in question is a baroque **palazzo** (Tuesday to Saturday 9am–12.30pm and 2–5.30pm) that was

49

Rococo fountain

The fabulous staircase

Inspecting the Roman mosaics

built by the Conde de Carvalhal in the 18th century. After his death in 1875, the palazzo passed into the hands of the Visconde de Estway. More recently, the palazzo has become the property of the city of Faro, which – despite restoration work carried out around 1900 – is busy wondering how to halt its steady decay.

The romantic palazzo ★ **grounds** are a joy. Stroll around the rococo fountain and among the moss-covered statues and busts of famous Portuguese and allow yourself to fall under their spell. It's fun imagining just how grand the staircase, with all its *azulejos* decoration, must have looked when it was first built.

The grounds have recently become host to Roman remains recovered from the ★★ **Vila Romana de Milréu** (10am–12.30pm and 2–5pm, closed Monday), an impressive site discovered in 1877 by the archaeologist Estacio de Vega. The finds on display include a lot of well-preserved mosaics, a 2nd-century villa with a colonnaded inner courtyard, domestic altars, a temple consecrated to the water goddess and also thermal baths complete with changing rooms and niches in which people would have taken massages.

The beautiful landscape alone makes it worth a detour to the health spa of **São Brás de Alportel**, and there is also the ★★ **Museu Etnografico do Trajo Algarvio** (Rua Dr José Dias Sancho 61; Monday to Friday 10am–1pm and 2–5pm, weekends 3–6pm) in an old manor. Not all exhibits are on display yet, but extension work is under way. The old stables with their saddles and coaches provide a fascinating glimpse into the daily life of previous centuries, and there are also several fascinating farm implements and costumes dating from the turn of the century. Cars can be parked on the road by the museum.

Route 7

Along the Border with Spain

Tavira – Vila Real de Santo António – Castro Marim – Alcoutim – Cachopo (111km/68 miles)

Portugal and Spain are divided by the Rio Guadiana. The tense relationship between the two countries is as old as Portugal itself. Spain has never really come to terms with the fact that its tiny neighbour went independent – and has remained so.

Today, the unloved Spaniards cross the border near Vila Real de Santo António, dressed in swimsuits and carrying shopping baskets. Things have improved: there was a time when they carried weapons, or cunning marriage contracts. The people of Tavira can tell you all about that.

Further up the Rio Guadiana the political distance between the two countries grows even more obvious. There are very few border crossings, and the connecting roads that do exist are of poor quality. Indeed, the border region is thinly populated. Ancient fortifications such as Castro Marim and Alcoutim are a common sight. The area is inhospitable and barren.

51

Northeastern Algarve and the Serra de Alcaria do Cume, once known as the Garden of Europe, is hardly recognisable as such, even right next to the Guadiana itself. The road to Cachopo passes through a primeval, rocky landscape, seemingly deserted apart from a handful of shepherds. This route is generally more suited to lovers of nature than lovers of culture.

Sandstone carving, Tavira

The finest town in all Algarve is ★★ **Tavira** (pop. 12,000) on the Rio Gilão. Its inhabitants are pleased not have been discovered by the tourist industry. The *Tavirenses* love sitting around in cafés, and they go about their business with all the calmness characteristic of Southern European people. Also known as the Venice of the Algarve, Tavira has numerous canals and bridges. The pastel-coloured patricians' houses, reflected in the river, exude a quiet elegance. You can really sense the wealth of bygone days. The roofs here (*telhado de tesouro*) have unusual pointed tops.

Tavira, the 'Venice of the Algarve'

The Gilão is spanned by the ★ **Ponte Romana**, a massive seven-arched bridge connecting the two sections of the town on either side of the river. A plaque at the centre of the bridge commemorates the successful repelling at this point of a Spanish invasion. This town has a lot of flair and more than 30 churches, many of which are worth visiting. Perhaps the most magnificent of all of the churches is the ★ **Igreja da Misericordia**, with its profusion of *talha* and *azulejos* decoration.

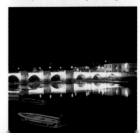

The **Ilha de Tavira** is the name of the island off the coast where the locals swim. The long sandbanks are good for surfing and also for children. In the summer a ferry leaves from Quatro Aguas every half hour. There is a further sandy beach, ideal for swimmers, just outside the fishing village of **Cabanas**.

The ferry to Spain

From Tavira it is 23km (14 miles) to **Vila Real de Santo António** (pop. 8,300), the border town with Spain. Spanish is the language one hears most often here. Fortunately, the bridge across the Guadiana was completed in 1992 so the appalling queues for the ferry – which used to be the only way of getting to Ayamonte – have disappeared for good. Vila Real has become a great deal more charming as a result.

The town centre dates from the 18th century and owes its existence to the Marquis of Pombal, the influential minister of King José I. Pombal had the town built in 1774 in the space of just five months – and it was clearly laid out and very functional. The chessboard pattern of streets were a direct copy of the plans Pombal had used to reconstruct the *Baixa*, the old town of Lisbon that was destroyed by the 1755 earthquake. The marquis is also to be thanked for the magnificent ★ **Praça de Marques de Pombal** in the centre of Vila Real, where the town hall and the mighty Igreja Matriz are also located. Vila Real is predominantly a town for shopping, though an important part of its income is derived from fishing.

Monte Gordo's beach

The neighbouring town of **Monte Gordo** (pop. 3,800) is essentially a fishing village that grew very quickly when tourism arrived. The concrete facades aren't exactly romantic. The whole place is rather like a cut-price version of Praia da Rocha, although the beach is impressive, with sand as far as the eye can see.

Castro Marim

The atmosphere gets very medieval when ★ **Castro Marim** (pop. 5,200) comes into view. The imposing 12th-century ★ **castelo** dominates the landscape for miles around. The Order of the Knights of Christ could have found no more favourable spot to settle: the view from the top is superb. There are traces of another, earlier fortress here, which suggests that the site is far more important than many believe.

In 1975, a large nature conservation area was set up in the marshland of the Guadiana Delta. Covering 2,089 hectares (5,160 acres), it is home to several species of bird including storks, cranes and herons. The ★ **Reserva Natural do Sapal**, with its marshy meadows and salt lakes, is a popular resting place for many migratory birds and therefore perfect for bird-watchers and photographers.

The route northwards from Castro Marim leads through a wild, solitary and impoverished landscape. Sometimes one passes the odd shepherd and his dog, dozing under a tree in the noonday sun.

If you feel like driving along the **Guadiana** past the fig and strawberry trees in its fertile valley, drive past the turn-off for Almada de Ouro and then turn right towards Alcoutim. The ruined *castelo* (formerly Moorish) in the small mountain town of ★ **Alcoutim** (pop. 1,300) reveals that the daily altercations, minor and major, between Portugal and Spain weren't always that harmless. It's no wonder this place has a population of only 1,300. The castle on the Spanish side, on the opposite bank of the Guadiana, is still pompous and magnificent. In the height of summer the heat slows everything down to a snai 's pace, and many people walk around with umbrellas to protect themselves from the sun.

Encounter near Alcoutim

53

The journey across the Serra de Alcaria do Cume leads past numerous areas of gorse, heather and rosemary. The moment the soil gets any damper, oleander can be seen. The best time to come here is in the spring, when the wild roses are in bloom.

Suddenly the picturesque little town of **Cachopo** (pop. 1,400) comes into view. This whole region is very remote, and any visits from outsiders are treated as a special occurrence. The town square is full of mopeds – the favourite means of conveyance in the Serra and indeed in most rural areas of Portugal. The old people putter along the country roads and through the villages at 20mph and these days many of them can actually be seen wearing crash helmets. The younger people love accelerating wildly. Cachopo is a good place for gourmets, by the way: it is famous for its game dishes.

Rural ride

Stripped asset

Route 8

Excursion to the Alentejo

Faro – Castro Verde – Beja – Évora (220km/136 miles)

The Alentejo is the granary of Portugal. Endless, golden-yellow cornfields cover the countryside as far as the horizon. The scene would be almost monotonous were it not for the olive trees, cork oaks and vineyards adding variety. Now and then a white point appears in the distance – a *monte*, one of the typical farmhouses, situated on top of a small rise.

The gentle contours of the landscape hide the fact that the Alentejo is one of the poorest regions of Portugal – mainly because of its aridity. Those who live here have to eke out a meagre existence, and many have long since fled to the big cities to escape the hard labour, unemployment and harsh climate. In this respect history is showing consistency. The Alentejo has always been thinly populated.

On the road to Évora there are two recommended places to break your journey – Castro Verde and Beja. Tourists are still regarded as something special in both these towns. In Évora, though, it's a different story: the town's many fine museums, churches and monuments attract culture lovers from all over the place, and there is plenty to occupy your time. You should plan for at least one night's stay.

By the way, the Alentejo is a treasure trove for anyone interested in crafts. Especially interesting are the colourful local ceramics which depict local customs and traditions.

ROUTE 8

0 _____ 50km

0 _____ 30 miles

Cross the Serra do Caldeirão and leave the Algarve, heading due north for Lisbon. In Almodôvar there's a scenic rural route which is well worth the extra concentration necessary from the driver. There are soft fields of corn to the left and right, and cork oaks and olive trees continually break up the scenery.

Almodôvar house

This part of Portugal has historically been known as *terra do pão* ('land of bread') on account of the numerous fields of wheat, oats and rice, and almost everyone in the Alentejo still lives off agriculture. However, you will hardly ever see anybody working in the fields. Unemployment is high in this region, not least because of a long period of serious drought. Formerly green hills are an arid yellow, and the earth is bone-dry. In recent years the crops have hardly been worth harvesting.

After the 1974 revolution many of the peasants occupied large tracts of land according to the motto *a terra à quem a trabalha* (land for those who work it). The Alentejo was at the centre of the agricultural reforms of those years, but today they have failed. The farmers have lost their fighting spirit in the face of the Lisbon government, competition from Spain, EU norms, and above all the persistent drought. In springtime, however, after the winter rains, the Alentejo landscape is often bright with red poppies, yellow gorse and violet thyme. The only relatively rare colour these days is green.

Castro Verde

The small market town of ★ **Castro Verde** (pop. 6,000) lies surrounded by cornfields and forests of gnarled cork oak. The highlights here include a small castle and a pretty church. The ★ **Igreja da Conceição**, built in 1713, is famed for *azulejos* which tell the story of how the Portuguese state was founded. This is an appropriate place for a Portuguese history lesson: in 1139, quite close to Castro Verde, the battle of Ourique took place at which Afonso Enriques defeated the Moors and became the first king of Portugal. The 16th-century ★ **Igreja das Chagas do Salvador** is also worth a visit if only to see its blue-and-white tile decoration.

You will probably see a handful of unemployed elderly men sitting together in the town's tiny marketplace, either chatting away or staring into space. This meeting place has a historical basis. Under the dictatorship the field workers used to gather here, waiting for the local *maioral*, or landowner, to come and hire the strongest among them to help him harvest. There is no such waiting nowadays: the young people travel to the Algarve to find work.

It is not surprising that the young are leaving the region. The whole of the Alentejo is gradually turning into steppe for lack of rain. The desperation of the local population is almost tangible. The church, which until recently had

An increasingly dry land

Heading home in Beja

Manueline ruins, Évora

Évora's Early Gothic cathedral

next to no influence in the Alentejo, is now organising processions to beg heaven for mercy. This appeal to heaven is significant: no-one has much faith that the government-planned Alqueva Dam project will bring much relief to the area.

The Romans had very few hills to choose from when they decided to build their fort – Pax Julia – in this region: the landscape is incredibly flat. Many years later the same hill – 228m (750ft) high and easily be spotted from miles away – became the site for ★ **Beja**, the capital of Baixo Alentejo province. The *castelo* in the town was built in the 13th century above the Roman structure. It is worth visiting the mighty keep, or **Torre de Menagem** (daily 10am–1pm and 2–6pm, in winter until 4pm). If you can manage the winding stairway of 197 steps you will be rewarded with a stunning view from the top.

At first sight Beja looks like a simple agricultural centre with rather nondescript buildings: it only yields its treasures on closer inspection. There is nothing sensational here, but a stroll through the streets of the old town will reveal a number of surprising details, including magnificent facades with high windows, Manueline portals, patios and doorknockers. Those interested in *talha* and *azulejos* (*see page 59*) should include a visit to the **Convento de Nossa Senhora da Conceição**. Built at the beginning of the 16th century, it has several interesting Manueline features.

The vegetation and the landscape on the road from Beja to ★★★ **Évora** (pop. 50,000) may be monotonous, but the capital of Alto Alentejo province has a lot of very special architectural treats in store. Within the old town walls there is a mixture of Moorish architecture, ruined Roman temples and Manueline magnificence. It sometimes seems as if the entire town of Évora is a museum. This was acknowledged by UNESCO in 1987 when it made the old town a World Heritage Site.

The best starting-point for a stroll through this fascinating town is the busy ★ **Praça do Giraldo**, which was also the centre of the town during Roman times. The square is named after Giraldo Sem Pavor (Gerald the Fearless), who captured the town from the Moors in 1156. The buildings here, with their arcades, columns and wrought-iron balconies, are quite magnificent – as is the marble **Fonte Henriquina** (Henry Fountain), which dates from 1571. At the top of the square is the Renaissance **Igreja de Santo Antáo**, with unusually simple, almost gloomy architecture for the 16th century.

The Rua 5 de Outubro leads directly to the town's imposing Early Gothic cathedral, the ★★ **Sé de Santa Maria**. It is the most important building in Évora as well as one of the finest cathedrals in all Portugal. With its massive granite blocks and its two asymmetrical defensive towers, the building gives every appearance of being a fortress. It's not surprising that it took from 1186 to 1330 to complete. The barrel vault inside is magnificent to look at, and also very cleverly constructed. The monastery next door contains an impressive cloister with statues of the Evangelists. Don't miss the **Museu de Arte Sacra** (Museum of Religious Art, 9am–12.30pm and 2–5pm) in the south tower of the facade.

A few steps further on is Évora's most astonishing structure: the Roman ★★ **Temple of Diana**. It was built in the 2nd century AD and is the best-preserved Roman temple anywhere on the Iberian Peninsula. How did 14 of the original 18 Corinthian columns withstand the ravages of time? It's quite simple: in the Middle Ages the spaces between them were walled up when the temple was used as an abattoir. In 1870 the temple regained its original appearance. Further southwest, in the Rua da Republica, is the ★ **Igreja de São Francisco** (daily 9am–1pm and 2.30–5pm), one of the most imposing Manueline structures of Southern Portugal. The nave, with its red stone inlaid with white, is simple yet elegant, and the walls, ceiling and pillars of the macabre ★ **Capela dos Ossos** are adorned with more than 5,000 human skulls and bones.

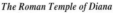
In the Capela dos Ossos

Typical of Évora is the Moorish-influenced *Mudéjar* style, instantly recognisable on the windows of the ★ **Casa Cordovil**. The house lies on the impressive Largo das Portas de Moura. At its centre is a 16th-century fountain with the stone armillary sphere of King Manuel I. Another building dating from the same time is the **Igreja do Carmo**, which has some intriguing Manueline 'rope-and-branch' carving on its portals.

The Roman Temple of Diana

Art History

Opposite: inside Faro Cathedral

Architecture

The Algarve has little in the way of early architecture. The *Reconquista* and the earthquake of 1755 ensured that practically all the noteworthy buildings in the region date from the mid-18th century or later. Some Roman ruins survive, notably the finds from Milréu (*see page 50*) and the remains at Évora (*see page 56*). Those historic structures that did survive were rebuilt in a manner that reflected contemporary taste.

There are a few ruined fortifications that remain from the period of Moorish rule. The castle at Silves (*see page 38*), the old Moorish capital of Algarve, was restored in 1940. The castle at Alcoutim (*see page 53*) on the Spanish border was modified by the Portuguese for protection against the Spanish. The mosques built by the Moors were systematically destroyed by crusading Christians, who built their own churches on the ruins.

Arab well, Silves Museum of Archaeology

59

For architecture unique to Portugal, seek out examples of the Manueline style. Originally referring to the reign of King Manuel I (1495–1521) it now more often refers to the whole of the Avis dynasty (1383–1580). In structural terms, Manueline architecture is Late Gothic. Its uniqueness stems from the overlaying of complex decorative elements. These decorations are often based on seafaring themes, for instance fishing nets, armillary spheres, or rope motifs on columns. In this respect Portugal's masonry reflects the importance of its maritime history and the optimism and wealth generated in the country by the Age of Discovery. Manueline elements can be found across the Algarve, especially on church portals, but perhaps the most concentrated collection is in Évora, which also boasts a 16th-century fountain with the stone armillary sphere of Manuel I, the king who gave his name to the style.

Manueline ruins

Talha dourada

The gilt woodcarving in many of Portugal's baroque churches is known as *talha dourada*, or just *talha* for short. It is one of the most typical decorative elements in Portuguese church architecture, and it dates from the end of the 18th century, when gold began pouring into the country from its colony of Brazil. Instead of paying off his country's debts by selling the precious metal, Portugal's wasteful King João V used it to decorate monasteries, palaces and churches all over the country. King, nobility and clergy lived far beyond their means in those days, and lovers of art today can be grateful that this was so. The finest example of *talha dourada* in the Algarve can be admired in the Igreja do Carmo (*see page 23*) in Faro.

Azulejos

Azulejos

The decorative sky-blue tiles known as *azulejos* are another part of Portugal's Moorish heritage. *Al-zulayi* (little stones) was the Arab name for them, and nowhere are these artistic mosaics more magnificent than in Portugal. Almost every church, monastery and palace contains them, but they are found particularly on inner and outer walls or as a border around windows. The tiles have a similar decorative function to carpets, tapestries or large paintings: strictly geometrical patterns alternate with motifs depicting fabulous animals, garlands, hunting or religious scenes. Some tile pictures are even sharply satirical. *Azulejos* have become quintessentially Portuguese.

Music

Folk music is all the rage: groups sing and dance to traditional instruments such as accordions, flutes, triangles, drums and bagpipes. The most famous dances are the lively *corridinho* and the more stately *baile mandado*.

The *fado*, a Portuguese lament, is not traditional in the Algarve. The singers are flown in from Lisbon.

Moorish influence

The Moors ran the Algarve for 650 years and their influence is everywhere, from architecture (*see above*) to agriculture. The Moors dug irrigation ditches, planted rice, and cultivated almond, fig, apricot, lemon and orange trees. They invented the *cataplana*, the simple pressure cooker used to cook typical Algarve dishes (*see page 63*). Moorish traces include words and names beginning with *al*; North African blue on buildings; and white-domed buildings. No wonder a Moorish poet said of the fall of Silves to the Christians: *Silves, my Silves, once you were a paradise. But tyrants turned you into the blaze of hell.*

Moorish Silves

Festivals and Folklore

Each year the Portuguese have innumerable festivals, *romarias* (pilgrimages) and processions. Most are of religious origin, and they usually begin solemnly. However, they are transformed into earthy and sensual affairs the moment the church services and the processions are over.

The most interesting festivals include:

Dressed for a festa

Albufeira   Festa da Nossa Senhora da Orada, 14–15 August. Fishermen carry the statue of their patron saint to the beach so that she can bless the sea. Market and dancing.

Alte   Festa da Fonte Grande, 1 May. A procession of *cavalhada* (riders), folklore groups and visitors makes its way to the Fonte Grande to celebrate water as a symbol of life.

Castro Marim   Festa da Senhora dos Martires, 15–17 August. A procession set against the backdrop of the beautiful castle. Fascinating crafts market.

Loulé   Romaria da Nossa Senhora da Piedade, Easter Sunday. A pilgrimage in which the statue of Our Lady of Mercy is carried into the parish church and worshipped for two weeks before being carried back. Astonishingly, the bearers carry the heavy statue at a run.

São Brás de Alportel   Festa de Pascoa, Easter Sunday. Carrying 'torches' decorated with flowers and singing 'hallelujah', a procession moves towards the local church.

Silves   Festa de Cerveja, third week in July. Beer festival near the castle, with much drinking and merrymaking.

Merrymaking

The markets (*mercados*) in the Álgarve are attractive because they are genuine local events. Spices, gold chains, cassettes, underwear and even various kinds of cabbage – they're all available at Algarve markets. Everything gets packed away at 2pm precisely.

The markets in Alcoutim, Loulé, Monchique, Olhão, São Brás de Alportel and Silves are particularly worth seeking out.

61

Food and Drink

Opposite: a taste of the Algarve

Fresh seafood and green wine

Portuguese cooking is filling and tasty. Particularly attractive are the numerous herbs and spices used in its preparation, many of which found their way to Portugal from its former colonies. For instance, the extremely hot Algarve chillis known as *piri-piri*, brought from Africa by the Moors, are just as much a part of the local cuisine as fresh coriander.

Nevertheless, restaurants serving regionally typical food are becoming a rarity in today's Algarve. The cooks are adapting to international tastes, and fast food outlets are springing up like mushrooms. That is not to say that everything foreign is admired by *Algarivos*. The eating habits of the tourists are a source of amazement to most locals: eating a mixed salad and some fruit at midday is definitely not their way of doing things. The Portuguese usually have a quick, light breakfast (*pequeno almoço*), a very substantial and prolonged lunch (*almoço*) between noon and 2.30pm, and supper (*jantar*) begins at 7pm at the very earliest. An extra meal before retiring to bed known as *ceia* is common after evenings out, and this can often continue past midnight.

Menus in the Algarve have a preponderance of fish and seafood, always freshly caught. The king prawns (*gambas tigres*) are so enormous that three make a complete meal in themselves. The menu may also feature unusual crabs known as *percebes*: these are cooked in salt water and are a real delicacy. Collecting *percebes* is very hard work as they have to be knocked off rocks with a small hatchet. Squid and octopus are best enjoyed freshly grilled and then sprinkled with salt and lemon juice and served with crusty bread.

The most famous seafood speciality of the Algarve, however, is the fish stew known as *caldeirada*. It's an absolute must for all visitors. Rather less complex but equally delicious are grilled sardines. *Cataplana* dishes – made with fish or meat and cooked in airtight copper pans resembling woks or pressure cookers – are always served for a minimum of two diners.

For those who have a sweet tooth, Portugal is definitely the right place to come. Sugar, eggs, almonds and cinnamon are just a few of the ingredients that are used to make an unbelievably wide range of high-calorie options. *Barrigas de freira* ('bellies of nuns') and *papos de anjo* ('angel cheeks') are two very popular desserts: they are a legacy of the Moors and the monks. The Algarve marzipan specialities are also excellent: try *bolos de doce fino* (marzipan with sweet egg filling), or *Dom Rodrigos* (marzipan wrapped in silver paper).

Catch of the day

Caldeirada

Sweet sensations

Choose from a range of good wines

The Portuguese are inventive when it comes to coffee after a meal. Purists don't just order an ordinary black coffee (*uma bica*), they ask for an *italiano* – it is black as night and not recommended for sensitive stomachs. Even the toughest of individuals will add plenty of sugar, however. A milder option is *carioca de café*, but remember to add the *de café* otherwise you may end up with a glass of lemon tea instead.

Portugal is famous for its wines, and it's worth sampling the reds or whites from regions such as Douro, Dáo, Bairrada, Borba, Reguengos and Vidigueira. One real speciality of the country is *vinho verde* (green wine). Containing just eight percent alcohol, it is light, fizzy and delicious on a hot day. In autumn, *vinho verde* is often served with a dish of fresh walnuts.

In 1980 the Algarve wines were divided up into four regions: Lagoa, Lagos, Portimão and Tavira. One of the best things about Algarve wine is its low price. It's also very strong, often with an alcohol content of 13 percent or more. Very low acidity is another hallmark. Very few of the wines are drunk outside the region, apart from those from the most important region – Lagoa.

Beer (*cerveja*) is by no means as popular as wine, but good brands are *Sagres*, *Cristal* and *Superbock*. Fiery spirits are distilled from carob (*aguardente de alfarroba*), figs (*aguardente de figo*) and the fruit of the strawberry tree (*medronho*). Those with a sweet tooth will enjoy the almond liqueur known as *amêndoa-amarga*. Mineral water (*agua mineral*) is extremely popular. It's thought to have healing properties, and some springs are even considered holy. The mineral water of the Algarve comes from the Serra de Monchique.

Set for supper

Here is a list of Algarve restaurants. The price guide is based on *à la carte* meals and range from expensive (**£££**) to inexpensive (**£**).

A feast in Albufeira

Albufeira
Castelo do Bispo, Estrada da Orada, tel: (089) 51 57 84. Good Italian food. **£££**. **Vila Joya**, Praia da Galé, tel: (089) 59 17 95. French. **££**. **Delicias do Mar**, Areias de São João, tel: (089) 51 50 39. Good food; closed Monday. **££**.

Alcoutim
O Central, Largo do Mercado 2, tel: (081) 472 66. **£**.

Aljezur
Ruth, Rua 25 de Abril 14, tel: (082) 985 34. Freshly-caught seafood a speciality. **££**. **A Rede**, Praia de Monte Clerigo, tel: (082) 987 59. Friendly beach bar that serves Portuguese snacks and desserts. **£**.

Almancil

O Tradicional, Estrada da Fonte Santa, tel: (089) 39 90 93. Expensive, delicious, and always very full, so reservations are essential. **£££**. **São Gabriel**, Estr. da Quinta do Lago, tel: (089) 51 57 84. An evenings only restaurant serving good quality food; closed on Monday. **££**. **Julia's**, Praia do Garrao, tel: (089) 396 51 21. Beach restaurant serving delicious poultry and lamb dishes. **££**.

Almaneda

O Poço, Largo do Poço 24, tel: (082) 694 33. Try chef Carlos's fillet of sole Algarve-style or roast lamb – they're both delicious. **££**.

Cachopo

Tia Rosa, Cabeça Gorda, tel: (081) 451 99. Good game dishes. **£**. **Retiro dos Caçadores**, tel: (081) 451 99, the chef is fond of hunting and so the game dishes are especially good. **£**.

Caldas de Monchique

Central, Rua da Igreja 5, tel: (082) 92203. Serves both regional and international cuisine. **£**.

Évora

O Gremio, Alcarcova de Cima 10, tel: (066) 74 29 31. Alentejo cuisine served in rustic surroundings. **££**. **Taberna Tipica**, Rua do Inverno 16, tel: (066) 275 30. Delicious and inexpensive local specialities. **£**.

Faro

Camané, Praia de Faro, tel: (089) 81 75 39. A good restaurant near the beach; its specialities include *caldeirada* and *cataplana de cherne*; closed Monday. **£££**. **O Bruno**, Rua do Alportel 94, tel: (089) 20 404. Good cuisine served at reasonable prices. **££**. **A Taska**, Rua do Alportel 38, tel: (089) 82 47 39. Delicious and inexpensive. **£**. **Centenario**, Largo Terreiro 4–6, tel: (089) 82 43 3. The food here is simple but good. **£**.

Ferragudo

A Lanterna, Foz-Arade-Parchal, 8400 Lagoa, tel: (082) 239 48. Delicious traditional dishes. **££**.

Lagos

Dom Sebastião, Rua 25 de Abril 20, tel: (082) 76 27 95. Excellent fish restaurant with brusque waiters. **££**. **Muralha**, Rua da Atalaia 15, tel: (082) 76 36 59. Serves regional cuisine and is open to 4am. **££**. **Antonio**, Porto de Mos, tel: (082) 76 35 60. Serves freshly caught fish grilled over wood coals. **£**.

Baking bread

65

Café in Évora

Al fresco refreshment, Lagos

Loulé
Aux Beaux Enfants, Rua Eng Duarte Pacheco 116, tel: (089) 620 96. Small restaurant with French cuisine. **££**.

Monchique
Charette, Rua Dr Samora Gil 30, tel: (082) 921 42. Excellent roast kid (*cabrito no forno*). **£**.

Olhão
O Tamboril, Av. 5 de Outubro 160, tel: (089) 71 46 25. Specialises in seafood. **£**. **O Lagar**, Pechao-Olhão, tel: (089) 71 54 37. Excellent squid and *cataplana*. **£**.

Portimão

Portimão
A Casa de Jantar, Rua de Santa Isabel 14, tel: (082) 22 07 82. Elegant restaurant with international cuisine. **££££**. **O Mané**, Largo Dr Bastos 1, tel: (082) 234 96. Popular restaurant, artists' meeting-place. **££**. **Escondidinho**, Porto de São João 22, tel: (082) 242 78. A lot of Portuguese eat here, so needless to say the cuisine is excellent. **£**.

Praia da Rocha
Almeida, Av. Thomas Cabreira, tel: (082) 270 75. Good seafood restaurant, crustaceans a speciality. **££**. **Fortaleza Santa Catarina**, tel: (082) 220 66. Good food with a great view, in the fortress of the same name. **££**.

Sagres
Carlos, Baleeira, tel: (082) 642 28. Seafood specialities and regional dishes. **££**.

Freshly landed octopus

In Silves fish market

Silves
Marisqueira Rui, Rua Comendador Vilarinho 25, tel: (082) 44 26 82. Good seafood, closed Wednesday. **££**.

Tavira
Quatro Aguas, tel: (081) 32 53 29. Delicious fish and seafood, terrace with view of lagoon. **££**. **O Alcatruz**, Santa Luzia-Tavira, tel: (081) 38 10 92. Freshly caught fish and seafood at reasonable prices; closed Monday. **£**.

Vila Real de Santo António
Costa, Sitio da Fabrica, Cacela-a-Velha, tel: (059) 95 14 67. Very good paella-style dishes. **£**. **A Camponesa**, Vila Nova de Cacela, tel: (059) 95 13 51. Delicious meat and seafood dishes in unpretentious surroundings. **£**.

Vilamoura
Taco, Aldeia do Golfe, Vilamoura, tel: (089) 32 27 18. Grill specialities; open from 9pm. **££**. **Akvavit**, Marina, tel: (089) 38 07 12. Fashionable with good cuisine. **££**.

Active Holidays

Golf

Portugal has some of the best golf courses in the world, and the finest are on the Algarve coast. Three top clubs are Quinta do Lago (36 holes), Vila Sol (18 holes) and Vale do Lobo (27 holes). All 16 courses are a high professional standard. Pine Cliffs, west of Vilamoura, has a famous 6th hole over the Atlantic. Contact Algarve Golf, Vilamoura, 8125 Quarteira, tel: (089) 38 81 99, fax: 38 91 53.

On Vilamoura golf course

Sailing, surfing and ocean fishing

Algarve offers most watersports, and equipment can be hired at major resorts. For windsurfing, contact the Centro de Windsurf e Vela do Algarve, Praia Grande, Ferragudo, 8500 Portimão, tel: (082) 45 11 15, or the Sea Sports Centre, Praia de Luz, 8600 Lagos, tel: (082) 78 95 38. There are modern marinas in Vilamoura and Lagos: contact the Marina de Lagos, 8600 Lagos, tel: (082) 76 27 65, or Condor de Vilamoura, Cais 1, Marina de Vilamoura, 8100 Loulé, tel: (089) 31 40 70. If you are intrested in deep-sea fishing, contact Docapesca, Armazém No. 4, 8600 Lagos, tel: (082) 76 18 20.

Speedy option

Beaches and water parks

Most Algarve beaches get a blue EU cleanliness flag each year. On the west coast the undertow is sometimes very strong and the water can get really cold. The *Aquaparques* (Esc1000–1500 per day) entertain for the whole day with pools, slides, waterfalls, playgrounds, dolphin shows, cafés and restaurants. Two popular parks are Slide & Splash, EN 125, Vale Judeu, Estômbar, 8400 Lagôa, tel: (082) 34 16 85, and Atlántico Park, EN 125, Quatro Estradas, 8125 Quarteira, tel: (089) 39 72 82.

Riding

Many hotels have their own horses or access to a nearby stable. *Hipodromes* have riding instructors and trained horses for lessons. The best time to ride is between dawn and noon. For further information, contact the Centro de Equitação Vale Navio, Estrada de Branqueira, 8200 Albufeira, tel: (089) 58 65 59, or the Centro de Equitação, Quinta das Oliveiras, 8800 Tavira, tel: (081) 22107.

A great way to spend a morning

Hiking

Discovering the Algarve on foot is increasingly popular. Many travel agents organise hiking holidays. The best tours can be found around Mount Fóia in the Serra de Monchique, and near Silves, Alte and Moncarapacho. New environmental regulations are in force, so be careful not to leave the paths; sand dunes are also out of bounds.

Getting There

By air

TAP Air Portugal is Portugal's national airline and it has wide international links. There are direct TAP flights from London Heathrow to Faro, Algarve, operating daily until the end of October and on Thursday, Friday, Saturday and Sunday from November to the end of March. For details, tel: (0171) 828 0262.

TAP also flies from JFK (New York) and Newark (New Jersey) in the United States, but travellers to the Algarve will have to change at Lisbon. For details, tel: (212) 459 0210 or (201) 344 3490.

British Airways flies approximately twice daily to Faro throughout the year. For information, tel: 0345 222 111. There are also many charter flights to the Algarve, whose prices vary enormously. Most charter flights are offered by companies in London; advertisements can be found in the travel section of most magazines and newspapers. Be prepared for a lot of shopping around if you want the best price.

By car

Drive carefully

Those planning to drive to the Algarve from the UK should allow a good three days travelling time. Don't try to save time on the journey: the number of road accidents is very high. Tolls are payable on most motorways in Spain, and a green international insurance card is essential. It is worth considering flying and hiring a car on arrival (*see below*): it may work out cheaper as well as saving time and stress.

By rental car

A rental car is highly recommended for those wishing to get the most out of the Algarve. There are several cheaper local rental companies at Faro Airport alongside the major firms. The minimum age for hiring a car is 21, and a passport and driving licence has to be shown. Fly & Drive arrangements are usually very good value.

By rail

Arrived in Lagos

Portugal is not yet linked to the superfast train network that runs in Europe, but there is a busy international and national service. A train runs daily from London Victoria: you have to change stations at Paris to travel on to Lisbon. The journey time to Lisbon is approximately 38 hours. From Lisbon you take the fast north-south service (Oporto – Lisbon – Faro).

In summer a Motorail service is available from Paris to Lisbon: your car will arrive a day later, so be prepared for a stopover in Lisbon.

Getting Around

By car

Road quality in the Algarve has improved noticeably in recent years. The motorway from Albufeira to the Spanish border via Faro provides good access to the most important resorts. The motorway is usually empty, while traffic on the parallel N125 proceeds at a snail's pace.

A lot of Portuguese get aggressive behind the wheel – so be prepared for unorthodox driving. Favourite sports include driving very close behind people at great speed and overtaking in dangerous places. The speed limit in built-up areas is 60kph (30mph), on country roads 90kph (50mph) and on motorways 120kph (75mph). Drink-driving regulations are very strict, and you could land in prison if you flout them.

In case of breakdown, call the *Automovel Club de Portugal* (ACP), Rua Rosa Araújo 24, 1200 Lisboa, tel: (01) 356 39 31, fax: 57 47 32. The 24-hour emergency-service number is (01) 942 50 95.

Petrol stations are generally open 7am–10pm, and 24-hours on the motorways. Lead-free petrol (*sen chumbo*) is available everywhere.

An excellent option

By bus

Bus traffic in the Algarve and to Lisbon is mainly organised by EVA Transportes SA. The network is comprehensive, and all country districts are well served. For further information call EVA, Rua Infanta Henrique 76, 8000 Faro, tel: (089) 80 33 22. The overland buses known as *expressos* are extremely comfortable. There's a daily express bus connection between Lisbon and Faro. The main bus station in Lisbon is in the city centre, at the top end of the Parque Eduardo VII.

By rail

The Algarve and Lisbon connect via the *combio azul* line, which runs regional trains (*Regionais*), *Intercitys* and *Interregioes*. If you plan to travel extensively by rail, buy a *bilhete turistico* for 7, 14 or 21 days of unlimited travel. Timetables (*guia horario oficial*) are available at shops and railway stations.

Taxis are easy and inexpensive

By taxi

Most taxis are still black with green roofs, but new taxis have to be beige in accordance with EU regulations. They are cheap compared to elsewhere in Europe. There is a surcharge of about 20 percent 10pm–6am and at weekends, and a 50 percent surcharge for luggage weighing more than 30kg is common. For long trips it is always best to settle the price in advance.

Facts for the Visitor

Time for a siesta

Chemists

Farmacias in the Algarve are usually open 9am–1pm and 3–7pm. A list of the nearest emergency chemists that are open 24 hours is almost always posted in the window of a closed *farmacia*.

71

For urgent medicines

Diplomatic representation

Australia: Av. da Liberdade 244, 1200 Lisbon, tel: (01) 65 41 61.
Canada: 2 Rua de Rosa Araújo, 6th Floor, 1200 Lisbon, tel: (01) 56 25 47.
Ireland: (consulate) 1 Rua da Impresa, 4th Floor, Lisbon, tel: (01) 66 15 69.
UK: (consulate) Largo Francisco Amauricio 7–10, 8500 Portimão, tel: (082) 41 78 00, fax: (082) 41 78 06; (embassy) 35–7 Rua São Domingos à Lapa, 1200 Lisbon, tel: (01) 66 11 91.
US: Av. das Forças Arnadas, 1600 Lisbon, tel: (01) 726 6600, fax: (01) 726 9109.

Festooned for festivities

Voltage

The standard voltage in Portugal is 220V, the same as in the UK. You will need to take an international adapter to fit the Portuguese sockets.

Public holidays

1 January (New Year's Day); Good Friday; 25 April (Carnation Revolution of 1974); Corpus Christi; 10 June (National Day); 15 August (Assumption of the Virgin); 5 October (Formation of Republic of Portugal in 1910); 1 November (All Saints' Day); 1 December (Restoration of the Kingdom in 1640); 8 December (Immaculate Conception); 25 December (Christmas Day).

Money matters

Banks open 8.30am–3pm Monday to Friday. Traveller's cheques and Eurocheques are accepted by banks when supported by a passport. Up to Esc30,000 can be drawn on a cheque. Foreign exchange outlets (*câmbio*) often have high service charges, so try an automatic telling machine – *multibanco* (MB for short).

Health

Travel insurance to cover medical care is strongly advised as the cost of healthcare is high. Medical treatment has to be paid in advance, but if you are insured then receipts for treatment can usually be refunded when you return.

EU Member States have reciprocal healthcare agreements, so UK citizens will have a large proportion of any medical costs met by the Portuguese authorities if they have the form E111, available from British post offices. Even so, this may not cover all costs, so travel insurance is still highly recommended.

There are hospitals in Faro, Lagos and Portimão. In an emergency try The Medical Centre (a 24-hour emergency service in Faro), tel: (089) 39 61 57.

Follow the signs

Tourist information

UK: Portuguese Tourist Board, 2nd Floor, 22–25a Sackville Street, London W1X 2LY, tel: (0171) 494 1441, fax: (0171) 494 1868.
US: Portuguese Tourist Board, 4th Floor, 590 5th Avenue, New York, NY 10036-4704, tel: (212) 354 4403, fax: (212) 764 6137.

Emergencies

For the fire brigade, tel: 115.

Policing the streets

For the police in Faro, tel: (089) 80 24 44, Lagoa (082) 52310; Lagos (082) 76 28 09; Portimão (082) 41 59 18; Tavira (081) 22022; Vila Real de Santo António (081) 43066.

Opening times

Shops are open Monday to Friday 9am–1pm and 3–7pm, Saturday 9am–1pm. Most supermarkets (*supermercados*) in the tourist centres open on Sunday.

Post offices (*correios*) are open Monday to Friday 8.30am–12.30pm and 2–7pm, though these times tend to change in smaller towns and villages. On Saturday, only the main post offices in Faro and Portimão and the post office at the airport are open. Postcards and letters to EU countries weighing up to 20 grams need stamps (*selos*) to the value of Esc75. Letters take about 5 days to get to most European destinations.

Telephone

Telephone calls can be made from any post office, or from payphones or cardphones. Phone cards (*cartoes de credifone*) can be bought at post offices and tobacconists (*tabacarias*). Note that phone cards bought in Lisbon and Porto are only valid for those cities.

Hotels sometimes charge as much as five times the basic tariff for phone calls. Many restaurants have payphones (look for the green-and-red signs). Reverse-charge calls are only possible from post offices.

When making an international call from Portugal, dial 00 followed by the country code (UK 44, US and Canada 1, Australia 61, New Zealand 649) and the telephone number. For the UK, omit the zero from the area code.

To call Portugal, dial the international code (UK 00, US and Canada 011) followed by 351 for Portugal, followed by the number. Omit the zero from the area code.

Service with a smile

Tipping

Service charges are included in the price. However, a small tip (about 10 percent) is appreciated.

Drinking Water

Tapwater is drinkable almost everywhere. There may be water rationing in some places.

73

Local brandy

Customs

There are limits for visitors from EU countries only on duty-free purchases: 1 litre of spirits with less than 22 percent by volume alcohol, 200 cigarettes or 50 cigars.

Toilets

Toilets in bars and restaurants can be used whether you are a customer or not. Keep some tissues with you.

Phoning home

Holiday village

Accommodation

Accommodation is classified from one to five stars and prices shown are always per room. All hotels are required by law to provide a complaints book (*livro de reclamaçáo*) for guests to use. It is also law that breakfast must always be included in the room price. The Portuguese don't eat large breakfasts, however, so don't expect a feast.

Hotels

There's no shortage of hotels in the Algarve, and the choice ranges from elegant and expensive to simple and good value. *Estalagens* are four- to five-star establishments. They are not quite as well-equipped as hotels (they may not have a pool or TVs in the rooms) but they are usually comfortable and typical of the region.

Pousada

Pousadas are state-run hotels, mostly of a high standard, in palaces, monasteries or castles in regions of historical or scenic interest. Guests learn about local culture in elegant surroundings, and the food and wines are usually excellent. *Pousadas* range from category B (simple) to CH (luxury). There are 36 in Portugal, but the Algarve has only two: in Sagres and São Brás de Alportel. Reservations are essential, since neither establishment has more than about 20 rooms. For more information contact ENATUR, Av. Santa Joana Prinesa 10, 1700 Lisboa, tel: (01) 848 1221, fax: (01) 80 58 46.

Country house holidays

Holidays in magnificent palazzos and country houses have become very fashionable, and they come under the heading of *Turismo no Espaço Rural* (TER). These buildings, often situated in splendid surroundings, have been restored for tourism. As the owners' paying guests, you can get a good glimpse into Portuguese life. There are 11 of these establishments in the Algarve covering three categories: *Turismo de Habitação* (TH) usually means country mansions with luxurious interiors; *Turismo Rural* (TR) will resemble a country-cottage holiday; and *Agroturismo* (AT) means farm holidays. Helping the owners with field labour or grape picking is much appreciated. Breakfast is included in the price. Reservations should be made well in advance. For further details contact either PRIVETUR, Largo das Pereiras, 49990 Ponte de Lima, tel: (058) 74 14 93, or ANTER, Rua 24 de Julho 1-1°, 7000 Évora, tel: (066) 74 45 55.

Holiday bungalows and apartments

Bungalows known as *Aldeamentos Turisticos* cater for all needs and are very well equipped. A large number of them can be found between Carvoeiro and Albufeira. They have restaurants, bars, shops, hairdressers and even domestic staff. The most popular accommodation in the Algarve, however, are the holiday apartments (*Apartamentos Turisticos*), which have restaurants, bars and swimming pools.

Holiday apartments

Boarding houses

Boarding houses, or *Pensões*, range from two- to four-star in quality. The rooms are clean, but they will be small and simply furnished and won't always have their own shower or bath. Boarding houses that don't serve breakfast are known as *Residenciais*. The most expensive form of boarding house is the *Albergaria*. These establishments are sometimes the only accommodation available in the less touristy areas.

Room with a view

Campsites

The Algarve coast has 22 campsites (*Parque de Campismo*) divided into four categories: those in category P (*privados*) are reserved for groups. Camping out rough is forbidden. Bookshops provide a good campers' guide known as the *roteiro campista*. For more information on camping contact the Federação Portuguesa de Campismo e Caravanismo, Av. 5 de Outubro 15-3°, 1000 Lisboa, tel: (01) 52 33 08.

Youth hostels

Youth hostels are known as *Pousadas de Juventude*, and cater for travellers aged 15–45. There are only three in the Algarve: in Sagres, Vila Real de Santo Antonio and Alcoutim. For more information contact Movijovem, Av. Duque de Avila 137, 1000 Lisboa, tel: (01) 355 90 81, fax: (01) 352 86 21.

Here are some hotels and boarding houses in the Algarve. The price system below is based on a double room with shower or bath for one night and ranges from expensive (**£££**) to inexpensive (**£**).

Albufeira

Albufeira
Alfa Mar, Praia de Falesia, tel: (089) 50 13 51. Large, modern, expensive. **£££**. **Boavista**, Rua Samora Barros 18, tel: (089) 891 75, fax: (089) 58 88 36. Quiet with sea view. **£££**. **Aldeia**, Av. Dr Francisco Sa Carneiro, Areis de São João, tel: (089) 58 88 61, fax: (089) 58 88 64. By the beach with two swimming pools. **££**. **Alfagar**, Balaia, Santa Eulalia, tel: (089) 54 10 07, fax: (089) 51 47 70. Comfortable Moorish-style hotel in a pine forest. **££**.

Aljezur
Residencial Dom Sancho, Largo 1° de Maio, Igreja Nova, tel: (082) 98119. Boarding house, small rooms. **£**.

Almancil
Dona Filipa, Vale do Lobo, tel: (089) 39 41 41, fax: (089) 942 88. Nice hotel with golf course. **£££**. **Quinta das Rochas**, Fonte Coberta, tel: (089) 39 31 65, fax: (089) 39 91 98. Country house with 6 pleasant rooms, cycle hire, 3km (1 mile) from the beach. **££**.

Alvor

Alvor Praia, Praia dos Tres Irmaos, tel: (082) 45 89 00, fax: (082) 45 89 99. Luxury hotel on the beach with swimming pool, riding, tennis, disco, etc. **£££**. **Golfe da Penina**, Montes de Alvor, tel: (082) 41 54 15, fax: (082) 41 50 00. Luxury hotel in a pine forest, very popular with golfers. **£££**. **Casa Tres Palmeiras**, Vau, Apartado 84, tel: (082) 40 12 75, fax: (082) 40 10 29. On a rugged coastline very close to the beach, swimming pool. **££**.

Caldas de Monchique

Caldas de Monchique
Abrigo do Lageado, tel: (082) 926 16. Recently re-opened luxury hotel, centrally located. **£££**.

Estói
Monte do Casal, Cerro do Lobo, Estói, tel: (089) 915 03, fax: (089) 913 41. Small British-style country hotel, good restaurant. **£££**. **La Reserve**, Estrada de Esteral, Santa Barbara de Nexe, tel: (089) 912 34, fax: (089) 904 02. Comfortable apartment hotel. **££**.

Évora
Pousada dos Loios

Pousada dos Loios, Largo Conde de Vilaflor, tel: (066) 240 51, fax: (066) 272 48. An opportunity to sleep in a four-poster bed with a view of the Temple of Diana. **£££**.

Convento de São Paulo, Aldeia da Serra, 7170 Redondo, tel: (066) 994 15, fax: (066) 99 91 04. Pleasant but not central. **££**. **Pensão Policarpo**, Rua da Freira de Baixo 16, tel: (066) 224 24. Rural boarding house. **£**.

Faro

Eva, Av. da Republica 1, tel: (089) 80 33 54, fax: (089) 80 23 04. Comfortable and expensive. **£££**. **Estalagem Aeromar**, Av. Nascente 1, Praia de Faro, tel: (089) 81 75 42, fax: (089) 81 75 12. Good beach hotel, 23 rooms. **£££**. **Faro**, Praça D Francisco 2, tel: (089) 80 32 76, fax: (089) 80 35 46. Centrally located and rather noisy, sun terrace on roof. **££**. **Casa Lumena**, Praça Alexander Herculano 27, tel: (089) 80 19 90, fax: (089) 80 40 19. Small boarding house in pleasant old mansion. **££**.

Faro's Faro

Lagos

Lagos, Rua Nova da Aldeia, tel: (082) 76 99 97, fax: (082) 76 99 20. Luxury hotel near beach. **££**. **Golfinho**, Praia de Dona Ana, tel: (082) 76 99 00, fax: (082) 76 99 99. Big hotel near beach, swimming pool, disco nearby. **££**. **Albergaria Casa de São Goncalo**, Rua Candido dos Reis 73, tel: (082) 76 21 71, fax: (082) 76 39 27. Small hotel in 18th-century villa. **££**. **Quinta da Alfarrobeira**, Estrada de Palmares, Odiaxere, 8600 Lagos, tel: (082) 79 84 24. Estate outside Lagos with pool and nearby beach. **££**. **Marina São Roque**, Estrada de Meia Praia, tel: (082) 76 37 61, fax: (082) 76 39 76. Small hotel with pleasant rooms, some with view of marina. **£**.

Loulé

Quinta de Benatrite, Santa Barbara de Nexe, tel: (098) 904 50. Comfortable country house 8km (5 miles) from Loulé, surrounded by almond and olive trees; reservations essential (only 3 rooms). **££**.

Monchique

Estalaghem Abrigo da Montanha, Estrado de Foia, tel: (082) 921 31, fax: (082) 936 60. Tasteful hotel with pool. **££**. **Quinta de São Bento**, Estrada da Foia, tel: (082) 921 43. Old villa with regionally typical rooms and excellent restaurant. **££**.

Hotels in Portimão

Portimão

Globo, Rua 5 de Outubro 26, tel: (082) 41 63 50, fax: (082) 83142. Pleasant and centrally located. **££**. **Vila Rosa de Lima**, Estrada de Torre, tel: (082) 41 10 97. Old estate with vineyard, four simple rooms, swimming pool, beach 2 miles away. **££**. **Pensão Miradouro**, Rua Machado Dos Santos 13, tel: (082) 230 11, fax: (082) 41 50 30. Comfortable boarding house. **£**.

Praia da Rocha

Algarve, Av. Thomas Cabreira, tel: (082) 41 50 01, fax: (082) 41 59 99. Modern, friendly, expensive. **£££**. **Bela Vista**, Av. Thomas Cabreira, tel: (082) 240 55, fax: (082) 41 53 69. Turn-of-century villa, pretty tilework, centrally located. **£££**. **Albergaria Tres Castelos**, Av. Marginal, tel: (082) 240 87. Clifftop location, quiet. **££**. **Solar Penguin**, Av. Antonio Feu, tel: (082) 243 08. Old boarding house on beach, noisy at night. **£**.

Querença

Quinta da Varzea, 8100 Loulé, tel: (089) 41 44 43. In a vineyard, riding, tennis, playground, cycle hire. **££**.

Sagres

Pousada do Infante, 8650 Sagres, tel: (082) 642 22, fax: (082) 642 25. On a clifftop with great view of Cabo de São Vicente, pool, tennis, golf. **£££**. **Fortaleza do Beliche**, Ponta de Atalaia, tel: (082) 641 24. Inside old fort, great view, restaurant not great. **££**. **Baleeira**, Sitio da Baleeira, tel: (082) 642 12, fax: (082) 644 24. Modern 3-star hotel in remote location. **££**.

São Brás de Alportel

Pousado São Brás, tel: (089) 84 23 05, fax: (089) 84 17 26. Set in mountain scenery outside town. **£££**.

Silves

Quinta da Figuerinha, tel: (082) 44 26 71, fax: (082) 44 42 26. Three apartments in a country estate with large orchard and swimming pool. **££**. **Vila Sodré**, Cruz de Portugal, tel: (082) 43 34 41. Family-run, good restaurant and wine cellar. **££**.

Tavira

Convento do Santo Antonio, Atalaia 56, tel: (081) 32 56 32. Old Franciscan monastery with 7 cells converted into luxury rooms. **£££**. **Quinto do Caracol**, São Pedro, tel: (081) 22475. 17th-century country house in beautiful grounds, small pool. **££**.

Vila Real de Santo Antonio

Guadiana, Av. da Republica 92, tel: (059) 51 14 82, fax: (059) 51 14 78. Comfortable, 40 rooms. **££**.

Option in Vilamoura

Vilamoura

Marinotel, Marina, tel: (089) 38 99 88, fax: (089) 38 98 69. Probably the most luxurious hotel in the Algarve, right by the marina; 400 rooms. **£££**. **Dom Pedro Golf Hotel**, tel: (089) 38 96 50, fax: (089) 69 38 95. Four-star hotel near golf course. **££**.

Opposite: Ohlos de Agua, near Albufeira

Index